What's So Special about Conflict in Nonprofit Organizations?

A S A LEADER[1] in a nonprofit organization, you have experienced on-the-job conflict: A staff member comes into your office and angrily fires off a series of complaints about a coworker. Unhappy with recent changes in the organization, a reliable volunteer suddenly decides to stop volunteering. Board meetings occasionally grind to a halt as two board members who have a history of distrust lock horns over an issue—any issue. Two program leaders have disliked each other for years, and you and everyone else can feel the tension whenever they meet. You don't know what their current problem is, but you hope it doesn't come to a head soon.

Though managing conflict was not the reason you entered the nonprofit sector, the fact is you are often faced with conflict in your work. The reason is that the nonprofit workplace provides the perfect conditions for conflict, according to researchers who study the subject. They identify the key factors that create conflict in organizations as change, diversity, limitations, and innovation—the very conditions in which nonprofits regularly work.

> Change. Changing government administrations, new federal programs, local disasters, harsh economic conditions, and movements in populations are some of the many factors over which nonprofits have no control, but to which they must respond. Further, internal change is continual for nonprofits. Staff turnover, changing composition of boards, new technologies, and new reporting requirements are a few examples of internal change.

---

[1] A leader can exist at any level in an organization. To be sure, special problems face the executive director, and this book addresses many of these. But this book can be used by anyone in a leadership role in a nonprofit, regardless of their designation.

"People who want to move things forward and don't expect conflict are expecting rain without thunder."

Zen master

Diversity. Increasingly, the people working in nonprofits reflect the people they serve. Work teams consist of people who vary in their ethnic, racial, economic, and cultural backgrounds, their individual world views, professional training, and personal characteristics, and their work and thinking styles. Diversity enriches nonprofits' abilities to respond creatively and empathetically to the people they serve, but also raises the potential for misunderstandings and conflict.

Limitations. With limited resources, nonprofits are expected (and expect themselves) to provide innovative, effective, and efficient services that address societal problems or maintain and enhance the community's cultural endowments. These conditions are perfect for conflict.

Innovation. Nonprofits often serve as the research and development laboratory for methods to expose and address society's problems. Social commentary provided by the arts and pilot projects conducted by human service nonprofits are but two examples of this role. Some people refer to nonprofit leaders as social entrepreneurs, and for good reason. The complex challenges and opportunities nonprofits face require the constant innovation that entrepreneurs are known for. The corollaries, of course, are constant change and frequent conflict.

Just as the shape of a sailboat and the materials from which it is built affect its speed and its performance, the structure of a nonprofit and the elements from which it is built affect conflict within it. The nonprofit's executive, board, staff, volunteers, service recipients, regulators, and funders all shape the organization. Each individual and group brings assets and concerns that differ from the others'. These differences are frequently the source of conflicts—turf battles between staff members; power struggles between board members or between board and staff; frustrations or secretiveness between foundations and nonprofits; or in arguments about program implementation or data collection between government contractors and nonprofit service providers. Precisely because decision making and implementation are dispersed among so many different people, we see lots of conflict over what things get done, how they get done, and who gets to do them. (For a capsule view of friction points in nonprofit organizations, see the tip, Rocks in the River: Typical points of conflict in nonprofits, on page 3.)

Beside the many internal and external forces that affect how a nonprofit does its work, two additional characteristics unique to nonprofits strongly influence conflict and how it is handled: first, leadership is shared between the board and the executive director and second, the expectation is that nonprofits are utopian agencies "above" conflict.

Shared leadership generates conflict. The board is made up of diverse people with diverse expectations, board members from other sectors often have goals or methods that differ from those of the nonprofit executive and staff, the lines of authority are often unclear, and the board is made up of part-time volunteers while the executive is a full-time, paid professional. Here's more about this constellation of problems.

Diverse participation. In recent years nonprofits and the foundations that fund them have worked hard to find board members who accurately represent the diverse communities the nonprofits serve. Though a multiplicity of viewpoints, experience, and expertise offers great benefits, it also increases the potential for disputes, debates, and full-blown battles.

Varied professional backgrounds. Boards draw their membership from people whose work experience is in other sectors—government and business. Many conflicts on boards and between boards and executives today result from the introduction of practices and values appropriate to other sectors but incompatible with nonprofits' legal and ethical foundations.

Vague responsibilities. By law, a board of directors is collectively the "captain" of the nonprofit organization and has the ultimate responsibility for its leadership. It employs the executive director, who reports to it. In fact, however, when something goes wrong in a nonprofit, it is most frequently the executive director and professional staff who handle the problem and whose reputations are on the line. The reason for this lies in the vagueness of board leadership: Though the board is legally chartered to steward the organization on behalf of the community at large, its responsibilities (and those of its members) are largely unclear and accountability for the quality of the board's leadership is nearly nonexistent. As a result, the level of stewardship provided by a board can range from lackadaisical to micromanagerial—either one a recipe for conflict.

The nature of voluntary work. Board members are part-time volunteers, which makes it nearly impossible for them to be deeply knowledgeable about the organization, its environment, and its services. Though boards have ultimate responsibility for the nonprofit, they steer them on a limited and intermittent basis. They must rely very heavily on their employee, the executive director, to keep everything on course and running smoothly, to educate and advise them, and to oversee the actual workings of the organization.

Rocks in the River: Typical points of conflict in nonprofits

Differences among board members in
- Personal and communication styles
- Vision for the organization
- Personal expectations of the organization
- Levels of participation in board work
- Understanding of board members' roles
- Amount of loyalty to the executive and the organization

Areas of authority and responsibility divided between executive and board
- Means of accountability for executive to board
- Degree of autonomy available to the executive in decision making and action
- Amount of information board needs to feel informed and do its work
- Level of policy making in which board engages
- Level of financial responsibility board undertakes to keep the organization solvent

Areas of authority and responsibility between board chair and executive
- Spokesperson role for organization
- Amount of information chair needs
- Evaluation of executive performance

Level of access to the board by line and mid-level staff
- Budget allocations between programs
- Personnel issues and grievances

Differences among staff
- Management styles
- Methods of program implementation
- Allocation of time and resources
- Personal and communication styles
- Expectations for participation in decision making
- Worker expectations for autonomy

Role confusion among executive and board members. The executive is the person who deals with all the daily issues, who is held accountable, and whose career is tarnished if problems hurt the organization. Most boards of nonprofits in trouble remain invisible and unaccountable. The dynamic of a part-time volunteer board managing a full-time professional executive holds the potential for many conflicts between the board and executive and among individuals on the board. In addition, as board leadership and composition change, the lines of authority and responsibility are also likely to change. This continual redefinition of leadership roles is built into the structure of nonprofit organizations.

The second unique feature of nonprofit organizations is the expectation that they and their employees are above conflict. Nonprofits attract creative, dedicated people who work long hours for modest compensation and believe ardently in their organization's mission. They believe that through their work in the nonprofit organization they personally contribute to the good of others. To a degree, they draw their identity from the work and reputation of the nonprofit for which they work. They view themselves as good, at least in part, because of their work in the nonprofit.

Ironically, nonprofit employees' creativity, individuality, and passion make them likely candidates for conflict. Their positive view of their work and themselves as "good people doing good work" leads them to assume that they will be above discord. Because of this belief many conflicts are buried and ferment until they surface again as complex and emotion-laden disputes.

In addition to expecting themselves to be above conflict, nonprofit employees often expect that the administration and management of a nonprofit will be "better"—less formal and more inclusive, entrepreneurial, and personal—than their counterparts in other sectors. Many nonprofit workers also expect that the nonprofit sector itself will provide a more flexible, informal, egalitarian environment than other sectors. Though this is sometimes true, many employees are disappointed to find that nonprofits can be rigid and hierarchical and bound by rules, policy, procedures, and precedent—all of which thwart their expectations of being free to do things their own way.

Whether you serve your nonprofit as a volunteer or professional leader, you assume many roles, some of which are contradictory. You may find yourself acting as a steward and advocate for your organization; a guide, problem solver, and advocate for the staff of your organization; and an advocate and activist for the community and the special needs your nonprofit addresses. Conflict management by a leader working in this context has limits, pressures, and responsibilities that differ greatly from those of external conflict mediators, who enter the organization for a short time to help with a particular issue and who have no special obligations to the organization and no ongoing relationships with the people in it.

What the nonprofit leader needs is a practical guide for handling most types of conflict internally, from the simplest difficulty to a complex, long-standing contention involving serious issues and many parties. That's what this book is. It presents basic information that can be immediately applied to conflicts in your organization. Its goals are to

- Help you understand some of the basic elements of conflict

- Provide an orderly way to think through the conflicts you encounter

- Offer skill-building exercises for developing the most useful and versatile conflict management skills

This book has six sections:

Chapter One has background information about the nature of conflict, including societal myths about conflict, individual responses to conflict, the nature of conflict within organizations, the impact of culture on conflict, and most important, the constructive potential of conflict.

Chapter Two presents the role of a conflict manager, cues for recognizing conflict, and a series of steps for managing conflict.

Chapter Three is the skills section. It explains and presents exercises for key conflict management techniques such as affirming, mirroring, reframing, and identifying interests. In addition it describes several techniques useful when conflict resolution seems to be at impasse.

Chapter Four discusses unusual conflicts: harassment, discrimination, illegal activities, and disagreements with the board, funders, or other groups that have special relations with your organization. Information about bringing in outside intervention, if necessary, is also presented.

Chapter Five focuses on what to do beyond intervention. It will help you introduce conflict management skills into the organization as part of board and staff development activities. It also discusses what to look for in your organization's systems and culture that create conflict or enhance conflict resolution capabilities.

Appendices include recommended reading, a bibliography, worksheets, and conflict resolution forms.

Throughout the book you will find sidebars that offer illustrative stories, quotes, and tips to augment the text.

In this book I frequently use images of the sea because I have always felt that the sea is a very apt metaphor for the way nonprofits work. Just as the sea teems with life in all levels of complexity, the nonprofit sector teems with diversity, new ways of addressing social needs, and people of great passion and commitment. As the ocean is the source and sustenance for living creatures, the nonprofit sector is the primordial brew of social betterment and change. Also like the sea, it is buffeted by forces that continually change its shape and direction. I liken the nonprofit leader to the mariner who must chart a course to a chosen destination equipped with knowledge of and reverence for the many elements that make the sea a life-giving yet unpredictable and dangerous realm. By virtue of your commitment to the non-profit sector, you are already a worthy mariner. My hope is that this book will offer you useful tools as you ply the seas of nonprofit leadership.

Bon voyage!

CHAPTER ONE

What You Should Know
Before Setting Sail

SEA CAPTAINS OF OLD had a great body of lore that helped them navigate treacherous waters and unknown seas. Some of these stories were based in fact and helpful. Others, based on superstition and outdated information, weren't. The nonprofit leader of today must grapple with a great body of lore that has grown up around conflict—lore both useful and harmful. Assessing this lore can help you understand people's reactions to conflict and thereby manage it constructively.

Be nice. Play fair. Don't rock the boat. From an early age we are taught that good people don't fight and must try to avoid conflict. This message is conveyed by the major religions practiced in North America, as well as by our education system and common parenting practices.

Our culture also encourages us to strive for the competitive edge and to field a winning team. Many organizational structures are based on those of the military, and in our language, sports and war analogies abound. We learn early to value competition—an organized form of conflict—in sports, education, and business, but are told not to engage in conflict in the family and in other organizational settings. We learn both to "turn the other cheek" and "go for the gold."

Sorting through these opposing messages is difficult. When should we engage in competition or conflict? When should we avoid it? We navigate these contradictions throughout our lives. While some of this navigation is helpful, much of it sets us on an unproductive, aimless course—one that can strand us on rocky shoals or leave us adrift in the doldrums. That's a tragedy, because one of the premises upon which these contradictory messages is built is really just a myth.

This myth is that conflict is negative and should be avoided at all costs. Wherever there are individual perspectives, interests, ideas, creativity, innovations, needs, desires, beliefs, and values—that is, wherever there are people—the potential for conflict exists.

Individuality, innovation, and the other qualities listed previously are highly valued in our culture and in nonprofit organizations. To have them, we must accept that there will be differences or conflicts. The very existence of competition and conflict can enhance these positive qualities. In an innovative, individualistic, and entrepreneurial culture such as ours, conflict is unavoidable and can be beneficial. Yet conflict is viewed as negative. This is a reaction to the negative behavior of people who are either trying to avoid or engage in conflict.

An important characteristic of conflict is that it is neutral. It is a fact of everyday life, including organizational life. However, when it is negatively handled, conflict can destroy relationships, eliminate or limit resources, and deny rights. Within an organization it can reduce productivity, hamper creativity, increase stress, and make organizational life a misery. Handled constructively, conflict facilitates creativity, defines and clarifies values and relationships, and even binds people who have weathered it together. All the characteristics we seek in nonprofit organizations—teamwork, a clear and unified mission, a supportive organizational climate, and innovation in service design and implementation—are advanced by dealing with conflict constructively.

Understanding Conflict

What is conflict? One widely accepted definition is

> a form of competitive behavior between people or groups under circumstances in which two or more people compete over perceived or actual incompatible goals or resources.[2]

This broadly accepted definition establishes two important qualities that exist in all conflicts. The first is the presence of competitive behavior. Competitive behavior arises when people view something as scarce or exclusive. The scarce or exclusive resource can be almost anything—the square miles of a nation or the square footage of an office cubicle. No matter what the scale of the scarce resource, the notion of scarcity leads people in conflict to adopt an either/or perspective and a belief that the result of competition will be haves and have-nots, winners and losers.

The fear of "losing" leads to behavior we commonly see and dislike in conflict situations—defensiveness, secretiveness, assuming knowledge, and attributing malicious motives to opponents, to name a few. (As you will learn later, a key task

"It is possible to conceive of conflict as not necessarily a wasteful outbreak of incompatibilities, but a normal process by which socially valuable differences register themselves for the enrichment of all concerned."

Mary Parker Follet, American management visionary, 1868-1933

---

[2] Moore, Christopher W. The Mediation Process: Practical Strategies for Resolving Conflict (San Francisco, CA: Jossey-Bass, 1986).

in managing conflict is to change the either/or perspective that drives much of the destructive behavior associated with conflict.)

The second key quality in this definition of conflict is incompatibility. Conflict happens when two or more people compete over perceived or actual incompatible goals or resources. Many conflicts are about differing perceptions. People in conflict often see the same situation differently, and their differing perceptions make their goals seem incompatible. (As you will learn later, an important task for anyone helping to resolve a conflict is to clarify the different perceptions held by people in dispute.)

As a nonprofit leader wishing to be a good captain, you must learn conflict management to increase the strength and resilience of your organization. To do that, you will need a basic vocabulary of conflict management—your navigational tools.

The Vocabulary of Conflict Management

You've already learned the first important tool in conflict management—a definition of conflict as a situation, neither good nor bad, that contains qualities of competition and perceived or actual incompatibility. This definition is your first step in divorcing yourself from the notion that conflict is bad. Following are a few terms that will help you understand the structure and elements of conflict.

Alternative Dispute Resolution: any one of a variety of processes designed to assist people to resolve disputes outside of the court system or other formal grievance processes. It is ironic that these processes are called "alternative" since the vast majority of disputes are resolved outside of the courts. People in the conflict resolution field often refer to it by the initials ADR.

Arbitration: an alternative dispute resolution process in which parties give a neutral individual or panel the authority to settle the dispute. Arbitration can be binding or nonbinding. Binding arbitration is not open to litigation; nonbinding arbitration can be brought to the courts.

Arbitrator: an individual who is given the authority by the disputing parties to determine the settlement of their conflict. The person has usually been trained to be a neutral third party.

BATNA: an acronym for Best Alternative to a Negotiated Agreement. It refers to the best possible outcome for a party if conflict resolution efforts break off or get stalled. WATNA is an acronym for the Worst Alternative to a Negotiated Agreement. It refers to the worst possible outcome for a party if conflict resolution efforts break off or get stalled. Both BATNAs and WATNAs serve as "bottom lines" that help parties understand their options and weigh potential resolutions.

Caucus: a private and confidential meeting between two or more people involved in the conflict resolution process. Any party in a conflict resolution meeting may ask for a caucus to discuss issues with any other person. Caucuses usually occur as independent meetings between a conflict manager and one of the parties.

Interests: the underlying needs or compelling issues of each party in a conflict. The interests are the conditions that need to be addressed for the parties to come to a satisfactory agreement. Interests generally fall into four categories:

1. Tangible objects like property or money (substantive interests).

2. The way something was done or a decision was made (procedural interests).

3. The emotions or interpersonal relations involved in the dispute (relationship interests).

4. The self-defined identity of either an individual or group (identity interests).

More than one interest is often present in a dispute. It is common to find that the concerns stated by parties in conflict mask some or all of their true interests, which are frequently left unstated. It will be your role as conflict manager to learn each party's true interests.

Mediation: an alternate dispute resolution process that is confidential, voluntary, and informal. In it an impartial outside person helps people develop a mutually acceptable agreement. Mediation is the least legalistic dispute resolution process and the one in which parties have the most control over the outcome.

Mediator: an individual trained to help people in dispute by using a structured process to communicate constructively and reach a mutually acceptable agreement. Mediators offer procedural help to people in dispute, but remain impartial regarding the interests of the parties and the agreement reached. Mediators sometimes are called neutrals or the neutral party.

Negotiation: the act of bargaining among parties who have a real or perceived dispute. Negotiation has two major forms. One is interest-based bargaining—a process that seeks to clarify and address the interests or concerns of all the parties negotiating. For example, in divorce mediation it is common to find that underneath the parties' discussion of asset division and child custody are their concerns for affirmation of their value as a person, parent, and life partner. The other form is positional bargaining in which each party takes a position that exaggerates its actual requirements for a solution and then gradually makes concessions until an agreement is reached. For example, when unions and management negotiate, each side often makes inflated demands (their positions) with the expectation that they will accept something less than the stated demand.

Party or Parties: individuals or groups of people involved in a dispute. Each person or group who holds the same interests or concerns is called a party. In everyday language we sometimes call these "sides." There can be two or more parties in any dispute. Parties are also called disputants.

Positions: solutions to a dispute generated by one party that satisfy its interests without necessarily taking into consideration the interests of the other parties. Note: A party sometimes describes its position as an element of a problem. For example, the statement "If we had more money, we would start that new program" includes a possible solution (more money) as a position embedded in the problem statement (inability to start a new program).

Power imbalance: a situation in which different parties have different degrees of power over one another. A person helping these parties develop an effective resolution to their conflict must be aware of power differences among parties and bring them into balance as much as possible.

These terms will be used throughout the book, so learning them will make for smoother sailing. Also helpful is an understanding of the basic structure conflict takes, a description of which follows.

The Structure of Conflict

Early seafarers told tales of fearsome monsters—giant squid, sea serpents, man-eating clams, huge sharks, and the Lorelei, who lured them to their demise against rock-strewn cliffs. Like sea monsters, conflict comes in many shapes. And though conflict can seem as random an occurrence as coming upon a sea monster, it actually has some structure to it.

Experts in conflict resolution have identified six categories of conflict, grouped by the types of issues around which they occur. (It is heartening that there are only six categories, but it is amazing how many different permutations exist within these categories.) The six categories are relationship conflicts, identity conflicts, data conflicts, structural conflicts, value conflicts, and interest conflicts. Recognizing these categories helps us analyze conflicts and design appropriate conflict resolution strategies.

Relationship Conflicts

Relationship conflicts concern the way people view and treat one another. They are frequently based on miscommunication, repetitive negative behavior, stereotypes, or misperceptions. They always involve high emotions. These conflicts often touch people's deepest feelings about themselves and others and cut to the emotional core of the people involved. Sometimes called personality conflicts, relationship conflicts are much broader than simple personality differences. In nonprofit organizations, relationship conflicts are often mixed with other types of conflict. And other conflicts may mask what are truly relationship conflicts.

I was once asked to mediate a dispute between a nonprofit day care and a small wholesaler located adjacent to one another in a neighborhood commercial district. The day care was particularly busy in the mornings and evenings when parents dropped off and picked up their children. The wholesale business had a lot of delivery trucks coming and going at the same hours. The owners were fighting over parking and snow removal.

The day care director was concerned that trucks delivering stock to the wholesale business frequently blocked parking for the parents shuttling their children. She was also concerned that the wholesale business owner did not shovel snow on his section of the sidewalk they shared. Parents carrying babies and toddlers had to struggle over piles of deep snow. Numerous complaints from parents convinced her that both of these situations were inconveniencing and even driving away her customers. She and the business owner had had several conversations about the situation, but always ended in a stalemate, with no action taken. By the time I was asked to assist, each had resorted to reporting the other for violations of city ordinances. Their city council member had finally been drawn into the conflict and asked that they mediate it.

It did not take long to generate workable options for snow clearance and parking. The wholesale business owner actually understood the impact these conditions were having on the day care business. However, he was unwilling to take any action unless the day care owner changed her way of communicating with him.

When the wholesale business owner spoke, his neck and face turned scarlet, but his words were measured and almost without inflection. When the day care director spoke, she was highly emotional. Throughout the discussions, the wholesale business owner chastised her for being "overly emotional" about the situation. Each time this happened she became more emotional and he became more monotone and measured. I finally called a caucus to see if we could get at the root of the conflict.

In caucus I discussed the communications style issue with each person. Although his words were outwardly calm, the wholesale business owner reacted strongly to his neighbor's expressive communication style (his flushing neck was a sure sign). He was extremely uncomfortable with the expression of emotion. His measured, mono-tone replies were an effort to control himself and the situation. He believed that the day care director's expressive manner was immature and unprofessional. He stated that her communication style was an indication of her lack of competence.

In caucus with the day care director, I learned that the issue of most importance to her was that she felt that both she and her nonprofit organization were devalued by her neighbor. His unwillingness to acknowledge how strongly she felt about her concerns made her feel belittled and discounted. She believed that he did not consider her responsibilities "serious" and was refusing to act in order to cause her organization to fail finan-cially.

Neither person was willing to talk much about their different communication styles and the relationship issue that lay be-neath the parking and snow removal concerns. They agreed to new snow clearance and parking procedures, but I left knowing it was a temporary solution. Their relationship conflict would generate new issues again and again.

It's nothing personal, but...

At first glance, relationship conflicts often look like substantive or procedural con-flicts. People generally hesitate to raise the relationship issue at the heart of the conflict, especially at work, where they feel they should rise above interpersonal issues. Intentionally or unintentionally, the parties mask the relationship conflict with conflicts about less personal issues that they would otherwise overlook. By the time the parties are uncomfortable enough to seek help resolving the conflict, there are often many issues layered over the relationship ones.

Identity Conflicts

Identity conflicts occur when people sense that the very essence of who they are has been attacked, belittled, or ignored. These are serious, difficult conflicts; resolv-ing them takes a great deal of discussion and mutual education between parties. Identity conflicts are often based on racial, ethnic, gender, or religious differences. When the values, practices, or beliefs closely associated with a person's self or group identity are either attacked or dismissed, the people involved in the conflict have the tendency to dehumanize one another. If you find you are working with an identity conflict, be patient. It will be a long, slow voyage to resolution.

Early in my nonprofit career I witnessed an identity conflict, before I even knew the word—let alone knew what to do about it. I was working with a number of people who had emigrated to the United States from a South American country. Some had come more than twenty years before and others were relatively new to the United States.

Strong negative feelings developed between the two groups, and they refused to work together. It turned out that the newer immigrants had stated that the more established immigrants were not "real" because they had assimilated some North American mannerisms and behaviors. The workers who were more established in the United States were very affronted that their national identity, which they viewed as essential to who they were, was being dismissed by the more recent immigrants.

Data Conflicts

Data conflicts are disagreements about information (data), its interpretation, its relevancy, procedures used to gather or analyze it, or any combination of these. Data conflicts are common when a nonprofit organization needs to justify funding based on certain data or when legislative or rules changes are being debated.

Some advocacy-oriented nonprofits have found that questioning the validity of their opponent's data, providing new interpretations of it, or questioning the procedures used to collect it are effective ways to get the media to cover issues important to them or to delay undesirable decisions. They use data conflicts as a technique for drawing attention to their agenda.

"We do not see things as they are, we see things as we are."

The Talmud

Data conflicts can be about the actual data, how the data was collected, or how it is to be applied. An example of a data conflict involving the actual data occurred when a local planning commission released figures about the effectiveness of septic systems. Environmental organizations used the data to emphasize the level of pollutants released by septic systems. Housing developers interpreted the same data differently, leaving the public officials torn.

An example of a conflict over how data was collected occurred during the development of a homelessness policy. For a study on how to improve services at shelters, researchers gathered statistics and interviewed staff at a number of homeless shelters. Recommendations were made to the legislature based on the data collected. However, when the study was presented, a group of advocates questioned the recommendations for services because no homeless people had been interviewed as part of the study. They argued that without gathering information directly from homeless people, the data was flawed and so were the recommendations.

Another type of data conflict involves how the data is applied. Our metro area has large communities of people from four different cultures in Southeast Asia. Researchers studied the largest group in depth and then tried to apply their findings to the other Southeast Asian cultures. The funders who wanted to assist these groups based on the research heard many objections. The groups argued that the data about one cultural group was not relevant or applicable to others simply because they all originated in Southeast Asia.

Structural Conflicts

Structural conflicts are about time (either too little or too much), organizational or political structure, or proximity. Many organizational conflicts result from the organization's structural systems. Some structural conflicts are intentional, such as checks and balances between different parts of a nonprofit regarding the expenditure of money. Other structural elements unintentionally result in conflict, such as the

differing fiscal years and budget planning cycles between funders and applicant organizations; conflicting deadlines for fund drives; or procedures that reduce the work
in one organizational unit while increasing it in others. Turf battles may be structural.
Conflicts between an organization's main office and satellite offices are often structural, as are conflicts within boards about the authority of board subcommittees.

For example, a multiservice nonprofit received many grants for a variety of purposes.
To track the use of grant funds, the finance department set up a series of project
codes to which staff charged time and materials when working on activities funded
by particular grants. A small group that handled public relations and media relations for all the different programs had access to all of the project codes. When they
worked for a particular program, they charged their time and materials to the program's project codes.

Program managers had no control over the public relations group and were surprised
and angered by unanticipated charges. Program managers and the public relations
staff often argued about the amount of time and the cost of materials used to develop
certain promotional materials. Conflict between the public relations staff and the
programs became so intense that many programs refused to use the public relations
service at all.

After years of arguments, turf battles, and finger pointing, two staff members—
a program manager and a staff member from the finance office—discussed the awful
state of affairs. They suggested changing the use of project codes so that staff outside
a program could not use the program's project code without the express permission
of the program manager. The structural change made all the difference. It took time
for the negative feelings to diminish, but the change in structure removed a significant source of conflict within the organization. And while "they all lived happily ever
after" would not be an honest ending to this story, things did get much better.

Value Conflicts

Value conflicts occur when one group of people tries to force their values or belief
system on another. We see value conflicts in our communities today concerning
abortion, censorship, and gay and lesbian rights. (Values are defined as the beliefs
that give meaning to an individual's life and guide decision making—for example,
what is good or bad, just or unjust, fair or unfair.) True values disputes are generally
irresolvable and quite emotional. A person's values and beliefs are so much a part
of their identity and self-worth that it's fruitless to try to change or negotiate about
them. Though peoples' values do change, they do so only when a person chooses
to change them. This is most likely to happen when a person gets new, meaningful
information that influences their ideas.

In a value conflict people often feel strongly that they are right and others are wrong—even to the point of believing that God is on their side. Issues are often viewed and presented in black and white terms, with no gray areas allowed.

In true value conflicts the only resolution is tolerance. People in conflict must simply accept that others' values are different and need not be changed. Disengagement is the usual resolution strategy. The results of disengagement without tolerance are miserable: they include segregation, discrimination, xenophobia, ethnic cleansing, apartheid, and isolationism—all of which breed further dangerous and destructive conflicts.

Occasionally value disputes can be worked through if parties share a higher value to the disputed one. They can sometimes settle their differences by emphasizing their shared higher goals. Sometimes this technique is applied in the creation of legislation, but the agreement often breaks down later when the subordinate values come back into play during rule making or implementation.

Figure 1. The components of an interest conflict

1. Substantive interests
2. Procedural interests
3. Relationship interests
4. Identity interests

When faced with an interest conflict, be alert for all substantive, procedural, relationship, and identity components.

Interest Conflicts

Interest conflicts are about actual or perceived incompatible needs or desires. Interests are the underlying needs or compelling issues for each party in a dispute. They need to be addressed for the parties to reach a mutually satisfactory agreement.

Interest conflicts abound, and most are resolvable. This type of conflict frequently has four components[3]—all of which need to be addressed for a long-lasting resolution. An interest conflict often includes substantive concerns about money, time, land, or other resources. There are also procedural concerns about how things get done or how decisions are made. There are relationship issues, like trust, respect, inclusion, friendship, and fairness. Finally, there are identity issues, which have to do with culture, religion, ethnicity, appearance, ability, or other personal characteristics; these often overlap with relationship issues. If a conflict resolution fails to meet any one of these needs, people are not satisfied and the conflict will continue or resurface.

Constructively handled, interest conflicts can lead to innovation and creativity. In an organizational setting, interest conflicts are likely to occur as the budget is being developed, in the allocation of staff time among programs, in discussions about compensation, or during a planning process.

---

[3] Christopher Moore, in his book The Mediation Process (San Francisco: Jossey-Bass, 1986), identifies three components of conflicts of interest that make up a triangle of satisfaction: substantive, procedural, and psychological interests. I have listed four types of interests, as have many other practitioners: substantive, procedural, relationship, and identity interests. Though identity and relationship issues can easily be viewed as subsets of psychological interests, they loom so large in contemporary life that I have chosen to treat them as separate types of interests.

I was asked to mediate the dissolution of an informal partnership between two nonprofits that had for several years run a joint fundraising and publicity event for their organizations. The event was the brainchild of the two organizations' directors, who in addition to being professional colleagues, had been close friends. Their professional and personal relationships had become strained, however, and by the time they asked me to help, they were angry and distrustful of one another.

Though the fundraiser had been a moderate financial success for both organizations, Director A stated that it was no longer worth cosponsoring: It was a drain on his staff and had limited financial return. Director B wanted to continue the fundraiser, which he thought brought both organizations financial gain and visibility. He also believed he needed an organizational partner to manage the event.

During the discussion, each director presented a long list of concerns about the mechanics of the event and disappointments and miscommunications between them. We discussed new ways to divide the proceeds and how to better organize the event. Throughout the discussion Director B tried to persuade Director A to continue the partnership. To that end, Director B was willing to take on more responsibilities and give a larger portion of the proceeds to Director A's organization. I was hopeful as the two directors developed ingenious ideas for improving the event and its management. But though the procedural and substantive matters seemed to be resolved, Director A would not bring the matter to a close. He kept raising old issues and questioning supposedly settled matters. Finally I had a private talk with him.

He told me that his own hurt and angry feelings were holding up the resolution. Over the years the media had profiled Director B, praising him as the creator and organizer of the event, and ignoring the significant contributions of organization A as well as Director A's role as co-creator. Director A felt that B had misled the media, hogged the limelight, and failed to acknowledge A's key part in the event.

With his permission, I talked privately with Director B, who said he had always noted A's important role, but the media had never picked up on it. He felt bad about it, but also felt that it was not his doing. I asked if he would discuss his feelings with his colleague, and he agreed.

Director B explained what had happened with the media, and his disappointment that they had failed to recognize Director A. But his tone revealed that his heart was not in his words, and Director A wasn't satisfied with the explanation. Despite the fact the event would earn more money and take less effort from his organization,

Beware the interest disguised as a value

Because many disputes masquerade as values conflicts, values disputes are quite tricky. Many people intuitively recognize that value conflicts are essentially non-negotiable; framing arguments as though they are true values makes it harder for opponents to attack. Calling upon "God, motherhood, and apple pie" can make an argument seem, at least initially, indisputable. Casting a dispute in terms of values, also, unfortunately, somehow enables opponents to view each other as bad, unworthy, or even subhuman. This is another reason values disputes, and disputes masquerading as values disputes, rapidly become personal and highly emotional. When people in conflict make values arguments, listen carefully for each party's underlying interests. This usually makes it possible to separate a true value dispute from the use of values as a strategy to accomplish some other goal.

Director A opted out of cosponsoring the event. Though they had resolved many substantive and procedural concerns, the two men could not resolve the conflict because they would not deal with the psychological element.

If the world were a neat and tidy place, every conflict would fit one of the six categories—relationship, identity, data, structural, value, and interest. But conflict often has more than one of these dimensions. As a leader and conflict manager you must sort through all the issues, stated and unstated alike. To do this, you can assess both by its type and its shape.

The Shape of Conflict

Any of the categories of conflict just described can take one of a number of shapes. The four most easily recognized shapes that conflict takes are direct conflict, spiral conflict, subtle conflict, and violent conflict.

Direct Conflict

Conflicts that are recognized and addressed by the disputing parties are called direct conflicts. They often yield positive outcomes in terms of the solution to the problem at hand and the relationship between the individuals in conflict. Though most people do not look forward to confronting a conflict, people who have resolved a conflict often feel a positive bond.

As the manager of a small arts program in a large regional planning agency, I had a conflict that worked as a catalyst to a positive relationship. The program, which supported small, community-based arts organizations, was the tiniest department in the organization. When a new attorney was hired, he decided to scrutinize the organization's programs. Focusing on my little program, he combed through its documents and guidelines for "illegalities." In several instances, I went to the mat with him about policies or practices he viewed as inappropriate and wanted changed. As a result some things were changed, but others were not.

About six months later, he asked me to serve on an organization-wide negotiating team with him. I could not imagine why he wanted a manager from this little program on the team. When I asked, he told me it was because of the way I had been willing to "take him on." We maintained a strong professional relationship and friendship for many years after.

Spiral Conflict

Have you ever been in a situation where people seem forever at odds? As soon as one concern seems resolved, another one pops up. In such a spiral conflict the people involved frequently raise many issues, but never get to their central concern, of which they may not be aware. They literally spiral around the source of the conflict as tensions, emotions, and frustrations escalate. This type of conflict is much like being sucked deeper and deeper into a whirlpool. Often it takes an outside facilitator to help people see the issue around which they are spiraling. Occasionally people who want to remain in conflict engage in a spiral conflict.

I once mediated a conflict between a custodial mom and a paternal grandmother. The mother and grandmother had two years of steady arguments about the mother's continual last minute cancellations of the grandmother's planned outings with her grandchildren. They argued about the types of activities, the means of transportation, the age appropriateness of different activities, the grandmother's health status, and on and on. Each time something was settled the mother had a new reason for denying the grandmother's visits. Throughout the mediation, the mother kept raising new objections to the outings—even when it was clear to everyone else that this was not the central issue. Finally, after much discussion it became clear that the mother was blaming the grandmother for raising a son who would leave his children. This was a classic spiral conflict.

Subtle Conflict

A subtle conflict is one in which at least one party refuses to acknowledge the conflict, even though the tension is palpable; even an outsider will sense something. It is common for the party that doesn't acknowledge the conflict to describe the party that does as oversensitive, imagining things, or paranoid. They may describe themselves as mystified or confused about the "sensitive" party's reactions.

A subtle conflict of this sort occurred when the chief executive of a small nonprofit hired a part-time program director to help start up a new program that had been the brainchild of the executive. As the new program director began work on the project she regularly sought the executive's direction on project goals and implementation. However, after a few months, when the project had begun to develop momentum, she found that whenever she set up a meeting with the executive, it was canceled. Instead, the executive would come looking for her on days when she was not scheduled to work. The executive complained that he was not being consulted enough and yet they seemed never able to meet . Soon, through body language and comments at staff meetings, it became evident that the executive was displeased with the program director. She asked the executive several times if he had concerns about the project or her performance. Each time the answer was no. However, the canceled meetings continued as did subtle signals at staff meetings that the project was not being handled well and that the program director was not a "team player." Her efforts to clarify the problem with the executive met with denials that a problem existed. The program director's discomfort with the situation became so great she finally resigned from the organization. She never did learn the true nature of the conflict that was hidden by the executive's claim of "no problem."

Violent Conflict

It seems almost too obvious to state that violence—either physical or psychological—is a manifestation of conflict. Violent conflict in the nonprofit sector is evident in the bombing of Planned Parenthood clinics and the murder of doctors who perform abortions by those who disagree with their actions. Workplace conflict resulting in violence between employees, or management and employees, is increasing as well. These are examples of the destructive, coercive shape that conflict can take, even in a sector whose self-image is one of societal betterment. But violent conflict can also appear in psychological abuse within the nonprofit sector.
For example, a small nonprofit organization had a long-running conflict on the board of directors. Eventually, one board member wrote a letter to the other board members alleging various improper and illegal behaviors by an opposing board member. The letter circulated in the nonprofit community, raising doubts about the person. This action was a form of psychological violence. Its goal was the same as that of physical violence—to disable or destroy an opponent.

How Individual Experience Affects Conflict

You can better understand conflict by looking at it through a variety of lenses. Thinking about the six categories and four shapes of conflict can help you sort out issues and understand how a conflict is playing out. However, other factors influence both the creation and resolution of conflict, including temperament, personal experience, family of origin, cultural background, and the individual's relationship with the dominant culture. In addition, each organization has its own culture, which also influences the experience of conflict. As you become more skilled in conflict management, you will find yourself taking all these factors into account.

We will first look at the ways in which personal experience influences how a person deals with conflict. Then we will look at the role of culture on both communication and conflict. Finally we will look at the role of power in organizations and its relationship to conflict. Understanding something about each of these elements can enable you to think through a conflict from a variety of perspectives.

How We Learn About Conflict

Most of us first learn about conflict and how to deal with it as children. Because household practices differ markedly, we each get a unique introduction to conflict and its resolution. In some households, spoken or unspoken rules state "no fighting"; disagreements are not discussed openly, and family members sometimes keep long mental chit lists of past wrongs. Other families view arguments as a means of engaging and entertaining people; debating or arguing for argument's sake can be part of maintaining family relationships. At the far extreme are families that use violence to deal with conflict. These examples illustrate the range of experiences that we, as children, have with conflict in our families of origin. These early experiences influence how we deal with conflict throughout our lives. In the heat of conflict, those same feelings and ways of dealing with differences tend to surface, no matter how old we are.

During childhood or later in life, each of us develops a preferred way to handle conflict. Knowing our own preferences can enable us to use them or switch to alternative methods when the situation calls for them.

EXERCISE

How did you learn about conflict?

To help others resolve conflicts, you need to revisit your own early experiences with it. Take fifteen minutes to remember what disagreements felt like in your family of origin.

- What emotions did you experience?
- What did you do? What did others in the family do?
- What were your family's spoken or unspoken rules about conflict?

Jot down your memories. The next time you confront conflict, compare the emotions you remembered feeling as a child with your immediate reactions as an adult. Though many of us have learned to manage conflict as adults, our initial reaction is frequently the one we felt as a child.

It may be helpful to expand this exercise to your work group. Differences in the way individuals view conflict can become a source of misunderstanding if they don't know that others can have a different, but equally legitimate, response to conflict. Invite your work group to talk about the conflict rules they learned as children. Kept light (and omitting names to protect the guilty!), such storytelling can help people understand one another when conflict arises. Exchanging stories is a good way to see how other people and families deal with conflict. It also helps people become aware of their unique experience. (People need to trust one another to do this exercise, so use it with care.)

How We Deal with Conflict

Each of us develops our own ways of dealing with conflict based on the family and social context in which we grew up. In addition our own temperaments also determine which style we find most comfortable. We tend to develop at least two styles—a preferred style and a backup style. Our preferred style is the one we use when we are calm and feel in control. Our backup style is often the one we use under stress or when our preferred style has been unsuccessful. Most of us are familiar with the styles that we prefer, but we frequently do not understand (or else undervalue) the other styles. The ideal, of course, is for each of us to be able to use many different styles, depending on the situation at hand.

Each style has its own strengths and limitations. Recognizing them can help you develop a successful strategy for resolving conflict between individuals with different styles, in the same way that understanding differences in coworkers' thinking processes or work styles can help you build an effective team.

In the 1970s Kenneth W. Thomas and Ralph H. Kilmann developed an assessment tool widely used to help people understand their own and others' behavior regarding conflict.[4] Thomas and Kilmann believe that, when facing a conflict, people use five major styles of behavior—competing, accommodating, avoiding, compromising, and collaborating.

Competing behavior: a style in which a person addresses his or her own concerns with little regard for the concerns of others. It is frequently associated with the use of power, winning for its own sake, or defending a position believed to be "right." It can be useful in emergencies, when quick decisions are vital, and when making decisions about unpopular courses of action, like discipline, layoffs, or budget-cutting in organizations.

Accommodating behavior: a style in which a person neglects his or her own concerns to satisfy those of other people. It can be associated with self-sacrifice and selflessness or with lack of assertiveness or fear. It is useful when a concern is of much greater importance to one party than another. It is often used when preserving harmony is essential. People also use it to establish social credits for future payback, as in "I'll scratch your back if you scratch mine."

Avoiding behavior: a style in which a person does not address his or her own concerns or those of other people. It is used to sidestep or postpone dealing with issues or to withdraw from a threatening situation. It is helpful when people need to "cool down" before addressing a conflict. It can also be useful to buy time to further analyze a conflict. When you sense that the presenting conflict may only be a symptom of a deeper one, temporary avoidance can give you the time necessary to determine what the conflict is and how to appropriately address it. Likewise it is useful when a person needs to gather more information before making a decision.

---

[4] Thomas and Kilmann's copyrighted assessment instrument, Thomas-Kilmann Conflict Mode Instrument, can be purchased from Xicom, Sterling Forest, NY.

Compromising behavior: a style in which people exchange concessions on less important issues to gain agreement on their most important ones. It is common when people are negotiating about some resource. It is particularly helpful in developing temporary settlements or in arriving at expedient decisions under the pressure of time. Because its outcome leaves all parties partially dissatisfied, it often serves as a fallback method of conflict resolution when collaborating or competing methods have been attempted but have not worked.

Collaborating behavior: a style in which a person tries to work with other people to satisfy the key concerns of all involved. It is useful when the issues in the conflict are too important to each side to be compromised. It requires a degree of trust so that people can explore each others' underlying concerns and creatively consider ways to address them. A means to innovative solutions, collaboration is effective when people must maintain positive relationships after the conflict is resolved.

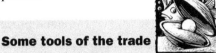

Some tools of the trade

A number of conflict style assessment instruments exist. If you are interested in learning more about your own and your staff's conflict styles, try one of these: the Conflict Management Survey by J. Hall, the Thomas-Kilmann Conflict Mode Instrument by K. Thomas and R. Kilmann, A Measure of Styles of Handling Interpersonal Conflict by M.S. Rahim, the Organizations Communication Conflict Instrument by L. Putnam and C.E. Wilson, and Communication Messages in Conflict by R.G. Ross and S. DeWine.

How Our Bodies Respond to Conflict

There is a knock on your office door and a head peeks around. "Can we talk?" asks a harried-looking staff member. With those words, yet another conflict has arrived on your doorstep. Ideally the person is calm and clear, but more likely he or she will be in an emotional state, usually sad or angry. In order to help, you need to learn the person's concerns. However, when an individual is upset, it is more difficult for them to give the information you need. With their brain in a state of emergency they can't be as fully articulate, reasonable, and creative as they usually are.

Physical responses. Your first step is to help the person calm down. To do that, you must understand the responses going on inside an upset person's body. When the portion of the brain that directly perceives the world indicates that something stressful or threatening is happening, it sends an alert to a more interior, ancient part of the brain, the limbic system, that simply says "There is danger."

This more primitive part of the brain makes no distinctions between types of danger: It responds in the same way to physical or psychological threats, and to minor troubles or major catastrophes. It works like an on and off switch. When switched on, it sends messages to prepare the body for fighting or fleeing. This automatic preparation works on our behalf when we are in physical danger, but it is often counterproductive when the "emergency" is emotional or psychological. Until the brain receives a message that the emergency is over, the limbic system overrides our more complex brain functions like reasoning and creativity. So when you are confronted by an emotional person, your first task is to establish an environment of calm, enabling the brain to sense that the emergency is over. Only then can the part of the brain that deals with language, reason, and creativity work to its fullest. (See Chapter Three, pages 88-93, for specific techniques for assisting upset people.)

Mental processes. The body's protective, automatic responses are not the only processes that inadvertently keep us from dealing well with conflict. Our mental patterns also pose some challenges. The brain establishes patterns as the result of experiencing repeated events or behaviors. Overall this is positive for our routine life activities, but it has a downside when it comes to dealing with conflict. When we encounter something new or different that does not fit with our previous experiences and established thought patterns, we experience cognitive dissonance—a sense of mental discomfort. The new or different perception is like a puzzle piece that just won't fit into our mental puzzle-picture of the world. The brain tries to find a way to force-fit the thought into our familiar picture. We may trim edges off of the new idea, or add new elements to make it fit. We tend to use our existing patterns to explain the new or different experience, no matter how implausible the explanation. The tendency to fit new ideas into already established brain patterns is called seeking cognitive stability.

What has this to do with conflict? A lot. It is common for people in conflict to experience cognitive dissonance. Their picture of the conflict is incomplete and often does not make sense. They know their own perceptions of the facts and their own reasons and motivations for action, but they don't know those of the other people involved. Their minds work hard to fill in the blanks to return to the state of cognitive stability. Unfortunately, people fill in the blanks by creating the information they don't know: their opponent's motives (usually bad) and personal characteristics (usually unappealing), as well as the probable outcome of the conflict (usually negative). Even positive known information about the opponent or conflict situation may get trimmed off as the person tries to make sense of the situation. At the end of an argument, have you ever felt hurt and said something like, "I would never have done _____. How could you have assumed that about me?" You are reacting to someone who, in the heat of conflict, trimmed off (temporarily forgot) established positive information from their mental picture of you.

Remember, conflict involves people competing over actual or perceived incompatible goals. As soon as a person identifies a potential conflict, they also sense a threat to achieving their goals. When people fill in the blanks in their understanding of this situation with negative assumptions and trim off positive ones, they make their understanding of the situation increasingly threatening. In turn, their bodies react as if they were in danger. These mental and physical responses make people in conflict defensive, secretive, and fearful. The result is that the real story behind the conflict is obscured by a cascade of protective physical and emotional reactions. One of the tasks of a conflict manager is to help people calm down, fill in the blanks with real information, and dispose of assumptions and false attributions so that the real issues can be resolved.

How Culture and Communication Influence Conflict

Not only are we products of individual temperament, unique life experience, family upbringing, and established mental patterns, we are also products of the culture in which we live or have lived. Culture establishes many of our communication patterns as well as our basic values—and often, these are so familiar that they are invisible to us. When not understood, these cultural patterns can be a source of conflict, particularly in the nonprofit workplace staffed by people from a variety of cultures. An understanding of cultural differences can be the key to conflict resolution, however. This book offers a brief overview of cultural patterns as a way to alert you to things to consider when you confront a conflict. The bibliography includes books that offer more in-depth information.

Note: The descriptions of culture here are generalizations used for example. Don't assume that a person from a particular background shares these general views.

The Role of Culture in Conflict

In general, people raised in non-Western cultures perceive and deal with conflict differently from people of Western European backgrounds—and there are plenty of unique characteristics even among different Western European peoples. Two key elements shape the way people from different cultures deal with conflict. First is a culture's shared beliefs and values about harmony and conflict. Second is the culture's communication style, both in language and gesture. These two elements are best understood within a broader framework that anthropologists use to view different cultures.

Geert Hofstede, a noted Dutch anthropologist, classifies contemporary societies on a continuum with two end points—collectivist cultures and individualistic cultures. In collectivist cultures, activities and decisions are geared to preserving and enhancing the cultural group. In individualistic cultures, activities and decisions are geared to preserving and enhancing the individual. Most cultures display a mix of collectivist and individualistic characteristics. These characteristics influence how people deal with conflict when it arises, and some may actually give rise to conflicts when people from collectivist and individualistic cultures interact. (See Figure 2.)

Hofstede based his approach on the work of Edward Hall. Hall, a scholar viewed as a major force in the study of intercultural communication, developed the concepts of high context and low context cultures and was the first to clarify some of the major communication differences between them.[5]

---

[5]   Hall, Edward. Beyond Culture (Garden City, NY: Doubleday Anchor Books, 1976).

Figure 2. Key differences between collectivist and individualistic cultures[6]

Collectivist Cultures	Individualistic Cultures
People are born into extended families that protect them throughout life in exchange for loyalty	People are born into an immediate (nuclear) family that offers protection largely through childhood
Identity is based on the social network to which one belongs	Identity is based on the individual and their ideas and accomplishments
Children learn to think in terms of "we"	Children learn to think in terms of "I"
Harmony is valued and should be maintained; direct confrontation should be avoided	Individual expression is more valued than harmony; direct confrontation is acceptable
Trespassing norms leads to shame and loss of face for the individual and the group	Trespassing norms leads to guilt and loss of self-respect
Employer-employee relationship is perceived in moral terms, similar to a family link	Employer-employee relationship is perceived in contractual/legal terms based on the notion of mutual advantage
Hiring and promotion decisions take the employee's social networks into account	Hiring and promotion decisions are based on individual skills and rules and disregard social networks
Management is management of groups	Management is management of individuals
Relationships are more important than tasks	Tasks are more important than relationships
Collective interests prevail over individual interests	Individual interests prevail over collective interests
Private life is open to the group; privacy is not a right	Private life is not open to the group; privacy is a right
Opinions are predetermined by group membership	Opinions are expected to be developed by the individual
Laws and rights differ according to the group to which one belongs	Laws and rights apply equally to all
Harmony and consensus in society are ultimate goals	Self-actualization by every individual is the ultimate goal
Communication is high context (see definition on page 27)	Communication is low context (see definition on page 27)

---

[6] Adapted from Hofstede, G. Cultures and Organizations: Software of the Mind. (New York: McGraw-Hill, 1991, pages 67, 73).

According to Hall, in high context communication, the message contains relatively little information. The people exchanging messages already hold most of the information, which they learn during the continuing acculturation process throughout their lives. They need and desire only the unique and specific information particular to the instance about which they are communicating. Japanese, Arab, and Mediterranean peoples, with their extensive information networks among friends, family, and colleagues, are high context communicators.

These cultures contain many communally accepted concepts, principles, and practices. Expecting to receive only unique and specific information from messages, people may view the inclusion of communally known information as patronizing or wasteful. For example, in a job interview in Japan, the job seeker will be specifically asked about family and friends in a job interview—the unique information expected from the communication. He or she will not be asked about skills, knowledge, or abilities because these are known, based on the reputation and status of the university the job applicant attended. In Japan, there is a known hierarchy of the quality and rigor of the education offered at different universities. The placement of the university in this hierarchy conveys information about skills, knowledge, and ability. Both university graduates and corporate employers know which university's graduates match the needs of corporations. Consequently, hiring decisions at Japanese corporations are primarily based on the applicant's networks—family and friends—the unique information about the individual. (Given these hiring practices, many new immigrants from Asia and the Middle East find standard hiring practices in United States organizations quite baffling.)

In low context communication cultures, relatively little communal information exists among the people communicating and much information is contained in the message itself. People in such cultures expect lots of information and data. Americans, Canadians, and northern Europeans tend to be low context communicators. For example, in a low context culture like the United States, it is expected that considerable background data and potential consequences will be presented to decision makers before a decision is made. Not providing this information, even if decision makers already know some or all of it, is viewed as careless or suspect (as though someone is withholding necessary information). Offering this level of information in a high context culture would be viewed as presumptuous, disrespectful, and a waste of people's time.

American, Canadian, and northern European cultures have the characteristics of individualistic cultures. Most South American and Asian cultures have the characteristics of collectivist cultures. When people from these cultures work together, it is important to understand different expectations about communications.

Here is an example of a conflict that arose specifically because of cultural differences. A large, Midwestern nonprofit employing over three hundred people hired a qualified individual who had been raised and educated in Central America. Her job was to facilitate the organization's communications with local Spanish-speaking communities. One of her tasks was to set up and document several community fo-rums to get input from Latino community members about issues on which the orga-nization worked. After six months, the employee and her supervisor discussed how the job was going. The employee was shocked to learn that her supervisor was un-happy with her performance: She had organized only one forum and had yet to write it up. Also a number of the employee's colleagues had complained that she continu-ally interrupted them to ask them to review and revise her written communications. They complained that they were doing her work as well as their own.

The supervisor thought the employee showed poor time management skills and a lack of task orientation. From the employee's perspective, she had made excellent use of her time. She had gotten herself appointed to three task forces in different Latino communities and had made many contacts over the past six months. She was also astonished at her peers' reactions to her requests that they review her written materials. Her understanding was that this is what professional colleagues do for one another.

Through lengthy discussion, the supervisor and the new employee learned how their cultures influenced their perspectives on the job. The supervisor and the other em-ployees were task oriented, while the new employee was relationship oriented. What peers had viewed as interruptions and avoiding work, the new employee saw as im-portant workplace relationship building and professional interaction. The behavior of all involved stemmed from their cultural perspectives about how to effectively get work done. Together, the supervisor and new employee decided how best to connect the organization with the Latino communities while respecting their different cul-tural contexts.

An exercise on page 29, Understanding cultural contexts, will help individuals and work groups explore how culture shapes assumptions about decision making.

The Role of Communication Style in Conflict

The second general element that influences conflict is communication, both verbal and nonverbal. While individuals from the same culture often have different per-sonal communication styles, they still share many culturally specific patterns of communications. A shared language is one. Even so, misunderstandings about the meaning of words are still a big source of conflict, even among people who share the same language. Several techniques for clarifying the meaning of language will be discussed in Chapter Three.

Though our choice of words can sometimes avert or create conflict, language is only one means by which we communicate. Experts estimate that 60 to 90 percent of communication occurs through vehicles other than words. Intonation, smiling and

EXERCISE

Understanding cultural contexts

In any group where people from different cultural contexts work together, it is wise to help people understand their own cultural contexts and recognize those of others before conflict occurs. It's particularly helpful to do the exercises that follow when a new group is forming or as new members join a group. They illustrate the cultural contexts from which people make their assumptions about how to make decisions or take action.

1. As a group, review and discuss the continuum of collective and individualistic cultures found in Figure 2. Ask each person to talk about where their home culture falls in this continuum and how a particular characteristic is evidenced in their culture of origin.

2. Copy and distribute the list that follows. Ask participants to choose from each pair of statements the one that best reflects their preference. Explain that these are forced choice statements, and that participants will probably not agree with either statement totally. Have group members discuss why they chose each statement and discuss similarities and differences in the group. (Needless to say, there are no right or wrong answers.)

I.

a) When making a decision, I like people to give me detailed information in advance. If I am not given detailed information, I feel uncomfortable or worried.

b) When making a decision, I like to get an overview and key factors. If people give me considerable detail, I feel they undervalue my level of knowledge. I feel impatient or uncomfortable.

II.

a) I think it is best to clear the air and confront people directly and immediately when I have a disagreement. Most disagreements are only resolved when people confront each other.

b) I think it is best to focus on getting along with people and to emphasize what we have in common. Most disagreements go away in time.

III.

a) I am most comfortable keeping my personal life and my work life separate.

b) I am most comfortable combining my work life and my personal life.

IV.

a) It matters more who you know than what you know.

b) It matters more what you know than who you know.

V.

a) It is critical to protect individual rights over community needs.

b) It is critical to protect community needs over individual rights.

The statements each person selects reflect basic perspectives that derive from the collectivist and individualistic characteristics of their culture and family background. In discussion, people begin to see that their cultural assumptions are sometimes invisible to them but are very evident to others. Recognizing and understanding your invisible assumptions is as important as understanding the assumptions of others.

laughter, pace, gesture, posture, eye contact, and physical distance all have culturally specific meanings. A gesture or expression that one culture views as positive, another will view as negative. Needless to say, it is easy to misinterpret nonverbal communication, particularly if we assume that other people's nonverbal communication has the same meaning as ours.

In regard to nonverbal communication, we are like the fish that doesn't know it swims in water until it jumps out. It is not until we try to communicate with people from different cultures that we learn about the nonverbal communication medium in which we've been swimming. Nonverbal communication is learned early in life, mostly by imitation and assimilation. Therefore we are largely unconscious of it. Our unconscious gestures and postures only become evident when they are not understood or are misunderstood.

As an example, consider how different people use their eyes when communicating. Americans of European heritage often look up and to the corner of their eyes when trying to recall information. This gesture indicates disbelief in several other cultures. Can you imagine how confusing this might be in a meeting between two people who understood these gestures differently? One person thinks they are conveying thoughtfulness, while the other person reads the gesture to mean disbelief. Most people are not even aware that they make certain gestures, let alone that they convey different meanings. This makes clearing up misunderstandings based on unconscious gestures a real challenge. An exercise on page 33, Mixed messages, will help you understand how gesture and language confusion can create misunderstandings.

Anthropologists who specialize in nonverbal communication estimate that the face alone is capable of creating 250,000 expressions. There are 5,000 distinct hand gestures possible. In all, the human body can produce about 700,000 different nonverbal signs.[7] Some say that many of these signs are much stronger than punctuation in writing or intonation in speech. (See the bibliography for texts that explain nonverbal communication in different cultures.)

Following is a brief introduction to nonverbal communication—just enough to alert you to these cultural waters. In the United States, where people of many backgrounds live and work together, individuals frequently combine elements from their cultural heritage with elements from the mainstream culture. As a consequence many people's nonverbal communica-

When words and gestures don't match

Even when all parties in a conflict are from the same culture, gestures can overpower words. I once facilitated a conflict for the members of a nonprofit board of directors. The board was making some difficult decisions about the future of the organization. Emotions were high and people had strong convictions about what they wanted the organization to become. One board member had the habit of smiling almost all the time. Even in the course of heated debate, he delivered his statements with a smile. He often said highly critical things about the staff and other board members, all through a big toothy grin. Because his nonverbal message contradicted his words, he caused a great deal of confusion among the people listening to him. Reactions of other board members and staff grew intense. They responded with anger and viewed the smiling board member as untrustworthy. He lost all his credibility with the board and staff because of his body language.

[7] Axtell, R. Gestures: Do's and Taboos of Body Language Around the World (New York: John Wiley & Sons, 1991, pages 10-11).

tion styles are based, in part, on how long they and their families have lived in the United States. This is further confounded by the strength of a person's identification with their cultural heritage. In other words, don't generalize from what follows; instead use it as a guide to learn more about the individuals with whom you associate. With this important caveat in mind, some generalities follow.

Space

North American people tend to stand about thirty inches apart (one arm's length) in normal conversation. In Asia, people generally stand farther apart, except for Chinese people, who generally stand closer than arm's length. Standing closer than the culturally comfortable distance can be understood as either aggression or intimacy depending on the situation. Standing farther than the culturally comfortable distance can convey disinterest.

Touch

North American people, along with many northern Europeans and the Japanese, are often not comfortable with touch among nonfamily members. Cultures for whom touch is much more casual and comfortable are those of most of the Middle East, Russia, Italy, Greece, Spain, Portugal, and most of Latin America. Greetings that include hugs or kisses, along with touching (generally between the same sex) during conversation, are standard ways to convey connection in touch-oriented cultures. The same actions can cause discomfort and negative reactions in cultures that are not touch-oriented.

Handshakes

Handshakes are recognized as a standard means of greeting in business throughout the world, even when bowing and other forms of greeting are standard in the culture. However, how people shake hands can carry unintended meanings. North Americans of European heritage value a firm handshake, which they interpret as sincere and forthright. American Indians, Middle Eastern peoples, and Asians prefer gentle handshakes, which convey peacefulness and nonaggression to them. To cultures that use a gentle handshake, a firm one can be misunderstood as aggression; to cultures that use a firm handshake, a gentle one can be interpreted as a lack of commitment or interest. In many cultures, handshakes across gender are not acceptable.

Don't assume anything!

As we become a mobile and global world community, it is even more challenging for a person of one culture to communicate clearly with one of another. Cultures evolve continually. As a result, people from different age groups within a culture have different cultural practices. For example, in Japan, many young professionals choose to shake hands rather than bow. They look directly into people's eyes, rather than between the bridge of the nose and mouth, as somewhat older Japanese people do. Regional differences also exist within the same country. For example, some African Americans are comfortable with direct eye contact while others—particularly those raised in certain parts of the South—feel that direct eye contact indicates disrespect or defiance.

Given these differences, how do we communicate effectively? The best answer is DO NOT ASSUME that a person's gestures have only the meaning you associate with them. Go slowly, clarify frequently, and remember, gesture is unconscious. Our own gestures can be as easily misunderstood as anyone else's.

Silence

North Americans are known for their discomfort with silence in conversation. Silence in a number of cultures—American Indian, Japanese, and Chinese, for example—is perfectly acceptable and viewed as showing reflection and respect. In these cultures, filling silences unnecessarily is considered rude.

A Japanese friend of mine, a professor of American culture, accompanied me to a faculty meeting at the university where I teach. He noted many differences between the ways in which faculty meetings are conducted in Japan and the United States, but an especially notable difference was the lack of silence in our meetings. At this meeting, as soon as the head of the department finished speaking, faculty members had many comments and questions. My friend explained to me that in Japan there would have been a long silence after the director spoke to demonstrate that the faculty were respectfully considering what had been said. Then, if my friend, a junior level professor, had questions or comments he would wait silently until all the professors who were his seniors had spoken.

Eye contact

Eye contact is expected and understood to indicate interest and forthrightness among European Americans, Eastern and Northern Europeans, and Saudi Arabians. However, in American Indian cultures, many Asian cultures, the West Indies, and Puerto Rico, the avoidance of direct and prolonged eye contact is a sign of respect. Similarly, some African Americans may avoid eye contact as a sign of respect. Misinterpretation of preference for eye contact can lead to serious misunderstandings between people of different cultures.

Smiling and laughter

Smiling and laughter not only indicate pleasure or happiness, but also surprise, embarrassment, anger, confusion, apology, or even sadness. In several Southeast Asian cultures and in Indonesia it is considered impolite to disagree with someone in public. Smiling and laughter can indicate the discomfort that comes with disagreement. In Korea, Japan, and Taiwan laughing with an open mouth is considered rude, so laughing is usually done behind a hand.

Gestures with hands, arms, and feet

Gestures made with hands, arms, and feet convey innumerable meanings. Here, however, are some of the meanings of common gestures:

- Arms akimbo (hands on hips) can be read as a very defiant posture in Latin America and Indonesia

- Hands in the pockets are impolite in France, Belgium, Japan, and Sweden

EXERCISE

Mixed messages

When my preteen says he's sorry with a tone of utter disgust, he sends a mixed message. His words say what he believes is required by the situation, but his tone and body language say that he feels anything but "sorry." The following exercise plays with sending "mixed messages" as a way to explore the strength and meaning our gestures carry. This exercise is a little like charades. One person is given a script containing words to say and also a gesture to accompany the words. The players try to determine which is the "real" message.

1. Say: I really like that!
   Gesture: It is repulsive to me.

2. Say: I agree with you.
   Gesture: I have my doubts.

3. Say: What do you think?
   Gesture: Nothing you say will change my mind.

4. Say: Very nice to meet you. I've heard nice things about you.
   Gesture: I've heard plenty of negative things about you.

5. Say: That is a very interesting idea.
   Gesture: Boring!

6. Say: Yes, I have a minute. What would you like?
   Gesture: Don't bother me.

- Pointing fingers is considered impolite by American Indian, English, Chinese, and Japanese people

- Showing the sole of the foot or shoe is highly offensive in many cultures of the Far and Middle East

Authority Figures and Conflict

A person's feelings about authority and authority figures also plays a role in the nature of conflict and its resolution. Like other aspects of conflict, personal beliefs about authority are shaped by culture. In many African, American Indian, and Asian cultures disputes are brought to elders, clan or tribal leaders, or religious leaders for resolution. In these collectivist cultures, authorities tend to seek conflict resolutions that restore harmony to the group rather than determine which party is "right." In America, most people look to an uninvolved authority figure to resolve conflicts and mete out "justice" or determine who is "right." The extensive United States court system, with its adversarial, competitive approach to determine rights and establish blame, manifests this focus—as do our tendencies to tell mom, the teacher, or the boss. Americans are notoriously litigious; many people are inclined to use legal or authoritarian avenues without ever attempting to resolve disputes themselves or with informal assistance.

There are strong positive and negative results from using an authority to resolve a dispute. The positive side is that presumably the authority is unbiased, knowledgeable, and can make a wise decision. Another positive is that when disputants do not like the resolution, they tend to be more angry at the authority figure and less angry at the person with whom they had the dispute.

On the downside, when an authority is used the relationship aspects of a conflict are rarely resolved. Disputants' underlying interests may or may not be addressed. Frequently, one or both parties feel dissatisfied and harbor long-lasting negative feelings toward one another. That's because most authorities deal only with substantive issues in a conflict, but leave other issues unresolved.

As a nonprofit leader, you are an authority figure to many people associated with your organization. Because of the cultural tendency just described, people are likely to bring you their conflicts to arbitrate. Employees, however, will often hesitate to do this for a while, because they want to be viewed as competent and self-reliant—characteristics valued in the workplace. So when a conflict comes to your door, you can assume that it has been going on for a while. You will want to weigh the factors discussed before deciding whether to shoulder the resolution yourself or whether to simply help the disputants work out a resolution.

In addition to expecting a leader to resolve conflicts, people who work in nonprofit organizations have attitudes toward leadership that range from deference to defiance. These attitudes may have little to do with the actual leader. Leaders' decisions and actions may be continually scrutinized and judged by employees, board members, clients, and funders. In addition, all sorts of assumptions and motivations get projected onto or against people in authority. All of this results in nonprofit leaders themselves becoming ensnared in conflict. While this book focuses largely on how a nonprofit leader can help others through conflicts, most of the skills and processes described here also apply when leaders themselves are engaged in conflict. So as you read, recognize that the concepts and skills presented apply whether you are managing the conflicts of others or managing your own.

Power and Conflict

Power plays a significant part in conflict, particularly in organizations. In a nonprofit, power is a force that drives and shapes the organization, just as designers "shape" a sailboat's hull to take advantage of wind power. Power in a nonprofit is shared, and many types of power are at work—all of which may be relevant to a conflict. How these types of power are distributed and used in a nonprofit influences its structure, governance, and culture.

The type of power most people first think of in regard to organizations is formal power, the power assigned to people by the organization. Because formal power is closely associated with status and resources, we mistakenly attribute tangible characteristics to it, as if it were a commodity. We assume that it is finite and fixed, but in actuality power of all kinds is always in flux and relational. In other words, a person only has power if another person accedes to it.

Formal power is an individual's assigned authority to make decisions, expend resources, provide rewards and sanctions, and represent the organization. Managers have significant power over the quality of their employees' work lives and careers. The board, when it chooses, has significant power over all aspects of a nonprofit, including hiring and firing power over the executive. The financial staff has power over program staff in regard to the use of resources. The development and marketing staffs' power comes from their ability to communicate with funding resources and constituents. Program staff and volunteers have power over the organization's service recipients and over the way the organization is represented to the community. These are all assigned, formal powers. But there are several other types of power not as readily acknowledged in the formal organizational structure.

While only certain individuals have assigned formal power, many people have various forms of informal power. Friendships, networks, and alliances among individuals in the organization create the informal power system. For example, I once worked in an organization with a very striking difference in formal and informal power systems. A shipping clerk with very narrow responsibilities and little formal authority was well networked throughout the organization and had strong political connections with powerful individuals who had external authority over the organization. He overtly demonstrated his informal power by frequently getting involved in decisions for which he had no authority and little expertise. The organization tolerated this because everyone knew of his extensive informal power—everyone but me, who, as a new employee, crossed him and learned about informal power the hard way!

A more vivid example of the difference between formal and informal power occurred at a high tech company in England. The owners of this successful, moderate-size business were negotiating its sale to a large corporation. Because of its profitability and quality, the organization commanded a high sale price. During negotiations the rumor mill ran nonstop among the company's employees. Morale was terrible and people were feeling scared and powerless about their company and their personal futures. One employee suggested to his colleagues that they had significant power to influence or even stop the sale because their combined expertise was, by far, the largest asset of the organization. He persuaded his colleagues to quit en masse should the buyout occur. They informed the buyers of their intent and the deal fell through. Although the company's employees had no formal power regarding the sale of the business, they used the power they did have—their expertise as a business asset—to stop the sale. It is likely that neither the owners, the buyers, nor the majority of employees recognized that the owners' power to command a high price for the organization was directly related to the employees' expertise (and therefore power) as a key organizational asset.

Assessing and balancing all the powers in a conflict is an important aspect of conflict management. In a nonprofit organization, the classic conflict between a supervisor and an employee involves an unequal distribution of formal power. The supervisor is vested by the organization with power over his or her employees' financial well-being and career development. No matter how kind, ethical, and professional the supervisor, the fear of misuse of this power often keeps a conflict below decks until one party can no longer tolerate it. (Note: when supervisors grossly misuse their power, their behaviors may constitute forms of harassment that need to be handled in very specific ways. Chapter Four has specific information on how to handle harassment.)

As a nonprofit leader, you must be creative about how to equalize power in a conflict. This does not mean that people will be peers outside of the conflict resolution setting or for the long term. It means you must create conditions that make it physically and psychologically safe for people to participate in conflict resolution processes without fear that power will be misused during the process or afterward. Understanding power differences is especially useful in three phases of dealing with conflict—in analyzing it, in designing the resolution process, and in managing the actual resolution dialogue. In Chapter Two I will describe practical ways to do this.

Figure 3. Types of power available to parties in dispute

- Formal power
- Expertise or information power
- Associational or referent power
- Resource power
- Procedural power
- Personal or charismatic power
- Moral power
- Habitual or status quo power
- Sanction power
- Nuisance power

Following are descriptions of various forms of power. You may not have consciously named them, but you are likely to recognize them and their use from your life experiences.

Formal power. This is the power that an organization bestows on a person by virtue of his or her position. It is usually identifiable by the person's title, the number of people and level of resources they direct, and their authority to reward and sanction employees.

Expertise power. This is knowledge as power, and is sometimes called information power. People who have information or technical expertise have power over others who need, but lack, the expertise or information. For example, information systems staff frequently wield a lot of power because of their greater understanding of the computer systems on which others depend.

Associational power. This is power by association, also called referent power or affiliational power. For example, the secretary to a CEO usually has significant associational power. This power comes not only from people's perceptions of the individual, but also from the access he or she has to the powerful person and the information the powerful person handles. (The story about the shipping clerk also illustrates associational power.)

Resource power. This is power over resources, both financial and other types. It is jokingly referred to "the other Golden Rule: those who have the gold, make the rule." In the nonprofit environment, major contributors have resource power. Foundation staff also have significant resource power because they provide access to the foundation's resources. In the example of the stymied buyout, the employees recognized their expertise as resource power and used it to stop the sale.

Procedural power. This is the power to control how discussions or events happen. If you have ever watched a board member skillfully use Robert's Rules of Order, you have seen procedural power. A social worker who knows how to contact social service agencies and understands eligibility guidelines uses procedural power on behalf of a nonprofit's service recipients. People in gatekeeping roles in organizations, like accountants and attorneys, often use procedural power.

Personal power. This power, sometimes called charisma or charm, is based on the attractiveness of a person to others; it gives an individual a strong ability to influence others. There are a number of well-known religious and political leaders who demonstrate and call upon this power—but many other lesser known people use it as well.

Moral power. This is power based on widely held values. Arguments based on God-given rights or mandates, religious writings, or basic cultural values are examples of the use of moral power. Disputes over abortion and the defunding of the National Endowment for the Arts include the use of moral power.

Habitual power. The power of repeated patterns of behavior is subtle and not easily recognized. The phrases "We have always done it this way" and "If it ain't broke, don't fix it" invoke habitual power. Force of habit makes organizational innovation challenging. For example, habitual power is often used in conflicts in organizations that are considering charging fees for services they previously provided free. Similar changes, like spinning off programs, changing clientele, changing established procedures, or restructuring, are often resisted using the power of habit.

Sanction power. This is the power to withhold something that a person or group needs or wants. It is often used in formal power relationships (withholding raises, promotions, and so forth) but it goes beyond this. Clients of nonprofits hold sanction power, because they can use word-of-mouth to damage the nonprofit's reputation, resulting in loss of service recipients, funding, or both. Sanction power is found in the social dynamics within an organization too. Excluding individuals from lunches or other social events is a form of sanction power.

Nuisance power. This is the power of the "squeaky wheel" taken to the extreme. People gain nuisance power through continual complaints or demands that simply wear others down. Recently I was told about a nonprofit employee who was not given a raise because of poor performance. He badgered board members about it over and over again. After a year, the board granted the raise, just to get rid of the nuisance—not an advisable practice for a board!

At this point, you may feel you are drowning in a sea of information about conflict. Take heart! Remember the good news about conflict: Handled constructively, conflict facilitates creativity, defines and clarifies values and relationships, and even binds people together. All the characteristics we seek in nonprofits—teamwork, a clear and unified mission, a supportive organizational climate, and innovation in service design and implementation—are advanced by dealing with conflict constructively.

When you, as a nonprofit leader, assemble staff, board members, teams, or committees, you no doubt consciously convene people with different perspectives and areas of expertise. As a matter of fact, you likely seek out and value people for their individuality, creativity, and special expertise. Given this, it is inevitable that two or more people will value different ideas, see different ways to achieve the group's goals, or have different styles of communication or problem solving. These differences lead to conflict, but they also lead to innovation and creativity. Handled respectfully, diversity and conflict are tools for weaving a net of community-relevant programs and activities and for fishing for the best ideas. It is our challenge to use this natural conflict to advantage.

To turn nonprofits, evolving service demands, changing financial sources, and our human diversity to advantage, you must permanently throw overboard the myth that good people do not engage in conflict. Accept that good people surely do engage in conflict. View conflict as a constructive act and give people the means to differ constructively, and you will bring out the best ideas and develop trust that people can work out tough issues together.

The next chapter will provide you with specific steps for turning conflict from a painful, negative experience into a creative, positive one.

CHAPTER TWO

Maps and Charts
Practical Steps in Managing Conflict

THE FIRST CHAPTER laid out background information to help you understand how culture, communication, individual temperament, and power shape conflict. In this chapter, you will learn about the role a nonprofit leader can play in managing conflict as well as specifics about how to do it.

Ship's Captain: Your Role as Conflict Manager

Keeping your organization on course means not only assuring that the funding is in place and the organization's public image is well managed, it means dealing with the human relations associated with all aspects of the organization. Peter Vaill, in his book Managing as a Performing Art, says "All management is people management, and all leadership is people leadership…there is nothing that a manager or leader can do that does not depend for its effectiveness on the meaning that other people attach to it." He goes on to say that today's leaders must manage in "permanent white water," which is his metaphor for constant change.[8] And as explained earlier, change is one of the conditions that promotes conflict. So as a nonprofit leader, handling conflict in the ever changing environment in which nonprofit organizations function is inevitable and a key role you must play.

Happily, your role as conflict manager draws on many skills you already have—communication, understanding your staff and board members, and sensitivity to the climate and interpersonal dynamics of your particular organization. Now you

---

8 Vaill, Peter. Managing as a Performing Art (San Francisco: Jossey-Bass, 1992, page 126).

need to develop a few skills unique to the conflict manager role, which is what this chapter will provide. The exercises in Chapter Three will help you practice these skills before you apply them in a conflict management setting.

One caveat before we begin: You already have a sixth sense essential to good management—knowing when to insert yourself and when to get out of your staff's way. Conflict management calls upon this same sense. There is too much work to do for you to get involved in every disagreement. The steps laid out in this chapter are designed for tough conflicts, the ones that seriously disrupt work, do long-term damage, and don't readily "blow over." Day-to-day conflicts—little ones that come from the heat of a stressful moment—are worth noting and watching, but are better left for staff members to work out themselves.

Conflict never happens at a convenient time: your desk will be piled with grant guidelines, and you'll be in the midst of long-range planning, struggling with budget cuts, or trying to write performance appraisals. You'll likely feel that dealing with conflict is an intrusion or a distraction from your "real" work. But conflict management is part of your real work. So as you probably do many times a day, re-prioritize your work and enter the white water of conflict management.

Sometimes all people need is "a good listening to"

The workplace is full of small conflicts that quickly come and go as people apologize, change their minds, or decide that an issue is not really so important. However, for certain day-to-day conflicts (like ones you think will submerge and become latent conflicts) you may decide to offer a little help as a preventive measure. An acknowledgment that an interchange was difficult and a casual invitation to talk it through with your help over a cup of coffee or tea may be just the thing. Likely, this type of problem-solving session is a management activity you already know well. Here's a little checklist as a memory jogger.

1. Have each person explain their concerns from their own viewpoint, uninterrupted

2. Ask questions, get clarification to understand each perspective

3. Discuss what is important to each person about their issues

4. Generate ideas for ways to address what is important to the people (and the organization)

5. Select a satisfactory solution and decide how to put it in action

6. Pour a fresh cup of coffee and take a momentary breather

Many of the skills discussed in Chapter Three are just as useful in these quick sessions as they are when dealing with tougher conflicts using the more detailed process described in this chapter.

An Overview of the Conflict Resolution Process

In general, a conflict resolution process has two major phases. First, the people recognize and discuss their differences. Sometimes called the differentiation phase because parties identify their differences, people find this part of the conflict the most frightening and challenging. Discussing differences could escalate the conflict, further damaging an already strained relationship. Emotions are high, and often little trust exists between the parties. During this phase, your job is also most challenging. Without your guidance there is a real possibility that the conflict might escalate. To avert this and move the process along, you will need to apply all the roles and skills we will discuss in this chapter.

The second phase of the process makes the tension and hard work of the first phase feel worth it. Sometimes called the integration phase, this is the creative part of the process. Once all the differences are known (and many commonalities are discovered), tension decreases and people often become creative. Though the tension or emotion does not completely dissipate, the level of energy and excitement increases as people generate and test possible solutions to their problem. Optimism usually increases and relations generally improve. It can be an exhilarating time!

Parties in a conflict are consumed with their interests, positions, and emotions. As the conflict manager you are also interested in these, but you must focus on the process. You are the person who establishes and refines the process that can guide people to a resolution. The structure and guidance you provide can turn a seemingly unmanageable conflict into constructive problem solving. But to do this you must use your role and resources effectively. Losing sight of these can negatively affect how you manage the process and its eventual outcome.

As a conflict manager, there are six key tasks you must perform in any conflict resolution process you design:

1. You act in such a way that the parties perceive you as impartial and trustworthy
2. You provide an orderly process to discuss and address issues in the conflict
3. You establish a physically and psychologically safe environment for the parties
4. You make efforts to balance power between the parties when needed
5. You stimulate the broadest range of possibilities for a resolution
6. You represent the interests of your organization

Here's more about each task.

1. Be impartial and trustworthy

As a respected leader, you are already likely to be considered trustworthy and you may also be considered impartial (probably termed "fair" or "unbiased"). In a conflict resolution process you must at all times be perceived as not taking sides with one or the other parties. To be perceived this way means you must actively work to avoid misperceptions. Even if you do not take sides, but are perceived as doing so, you will not be effective facilitating a conflict resolution process. (For practical information, see the section on Asking Neutral Questions and Making Neutral Statements on pages 87-88 of Chapter Three.)

A second aspect of trustworthiness is helping the parties rebuild trust. One of the first by-products of conflict is distrust. People frequently ascribe bad motives, ill will, and untrustworthiness to the other party. As differences, assumptions, and needs are clarified and parties gain greater information about each other's concerns and perspectives, much distrust falls away. Rebuilding trust is a key developmental goal of conflict management. It is an investment in the future working relationship among the parties and goes well beyond the issue at hand.

In a conflict resolution process you must at all times be perceived as not taking sides with one or the other parties. To be perceived as impartial means you must actively work to avoid misperceptions.

2. Provide an orderly process

Through establishing a process for the discussion and resolution of a conflict you bring order to what feels like chaos to the people involved. You establish yourself as the neutral manager of the process. Activities such as establishing ground rules for decorum help people control their behavior and give assurance that others will do the same. Breaking the conflict into its component issues helps untangle the substantive, emotional, and procedural issues that often make conflict seem overwhelming and irreconcilable. (For more information, see the list of sequential phases of conflict resolution in Step 5: Design the Process, page 65.)

A sense of orderliness helps people feel less threatened. They can rely on you and their own willingness to participate in the process to govern their behavior. This does not mean that strong emotions and opinions will not be expressed. They will. But using an orderly process gives people boundaries and also helps them mark progress toward the ultimate goal of resolution.

Using an orderly process gives people boundaries and also helps them mark progress toward the ultimate goal of resolution.

3. Establish a safe environment

Rarely will you need to worry about physical safety when conducting conflict resolution in a nonprofit. Ensuring psychological safety is another matter, however. People in conflict have many fears. The conflict has usually been latent for some time, and emotions have escalated by the time the parties agree to participate in a conflict resolution process. Most people fear that they will say things that will intensify the conflict and make them lose face. You will learn more about handling people's emotions in Step 5: Design the Process. Parties also fear that the other party will embarrass or shame them. Therefore, setting up an environment of respectful interaction is important in establishing psychological safety. Tips on pages 76-77 in Step 7: Conduct the Process cover the rules for establishing physical and psychological safety during conflict resolution meetings.

Confidentiality is part of psychological safety and is often a complex issue. As a conflict manager you must keep strictly confidential any information you are told in private. So must all participants in the conflict resolution meetings. People need reassurance that personal and difficult issues discussed in private will remain so. Given the strong emotions involved, people fear that the other party, whom they distrust, will use private information to hurt them. Requiring confidentiality of all parties diminishes these fears and can improve the success of the process. In Step 5: Design the Process, you will learn how to set ground rules for confidentiality and how to impose sanctions against breaking them.

Some important exceptions to maintaining confidentiality exist. If a criminal act or instances of abuse, harassment, maltreatment of a vulnerable person, or some illegal actions come to light during conflict resolution, you will need to follow other processes and rules that govern these situations. These situations may not be held confidential within the conflict management process. In Chapter Four I will cover briefly these special cases and the processes to be used for them.

4. Balance power between the disputing parties

In the first chapter I discussed the many types of power that people in organizations have available to them. (See pages 34-37.) When one party has significant power over the other, you must create ways to balance the power within the conflict management process. For example, in a conflict between an employee and a supervisor, the employee will be concerned about potential retaliation by the supervisor. If you have authority over the supervisor in the conflict, then you may serve to balance the authority. (In this case, the supervisor will want to behave professionally in your presence. Your knowledge of the process and its resolution makes the supervisor accountable to you for living up to the agreement.)

Ways to guard against potential retaliation can become part of the resolution discussion itself. For example, the employee's performance reviews can be overseen by a third party, the employee can arrange check-in periods with the conflict manager, specific goals can be built into both the supervisor's and employee's work plans, the employee's reporting structure can be changed. Depending on the issue, the parties may be able to develop their own unique ways to assure compliance in their agreement. (More information on balancing power appears in Step 5: Design the Process.)

When one party has significant power over the other, you must create ways to balance the power within the conflict management process.

5. Stimulate possibilities for resolution

When people only know or consider their own needs, their solutions to problems are often limited. The differentiation phase of the conflict process (described in Step 5: Design the Process, on page 66) often brings to light considerable new information about the other party's needs and concerns. This provides the raw material for potential solutions. In addition, your optimism, confidence in the parties, and focus toward the future directs the parties toward resolution rather than blaming and fault finding.

The most common method for stimulating new ideas is brainstorming—simply listing all the possible ways the parties' interests can be met. It is useful because so many people are already familiar with it, so it takes limited explanation. Note, though, that brainstorming works best for people who value extroversion, time as a commodity, egalitarianism, and action over reflection.

Other idea-generating techniques may be more appropriate for people whose personality and cultural background do not favor brainstorming. After they know each other's interests, parties can independently devise potential solutions and then come together to share and discuss them. Many other ideas for stimulating idea generation are presented in the Breaking Stalemates section of Chapter Three on pages 105-108.

6. Represent the interests of your organization

Your organization has many constraints on it imposed by its financial situation, mission, internal policies and precedents, as well as by its funders and regulators. As an organizational leader, it's your responsibility to assure that the organization functions within these boundaries. Resolutions to conflicts within the organization must likewise be constrained by these forces. Therefore, you will need to give the parties guidance about the realities of the organization's limitations and the viability of their proposed solutions. This makes you different from an external conflict manager who can oversee a conflict resolution process without having a stake in its outcome. As a steward of your organization you do have a stake.

For example, parties may develop a solution that runs counter to existing organizational policy or procedure. Though it is worthwhile to weigh the importance of maintaining the policy or procedure—they do become outmoded—you may find that the proposed solution is not in the best interests of the organization. At that point you will need to help the parties consider other options that meet their interests and those of the organization. Likewise, some optimal solutions are beyond the resources of the organization. This too means reconsidering the parties' solutions. (For more information, see Step 4: Analyze the Conflict, pages 53-64.)

When the conflict includes you

Most of this book focuses on your leadership role in helping manage conflicts so that they improve the organization. But no one is free from conflict. Inevitably, conflicts will involve you as well.

All of the concepts and skills offered in this book will help you when you are part of the conflict, but they are much more difficult to apply. As with any person in a conflict, your emotions will hinder your objectivity. Practice the exercises in this book, know your typical physical and emotional responses, and use whatever works to calm yourself.

Find time to analyze the conflict, using the steps and worksheets provided in this book. Just keep in mind that you can't be truly impartial in this situation. If the conflict is one which you can handle directly with the other people involved, then do so. If not, find help elsewhere, either in the organization or outside of it. Most work conflicts can be resolved fairly easily and quickly, especially if you avoid getting hooked into the other person's emotional responses.

Setting Sail: The Steps in Designing and Conducting a Conflict Resolution Process

Every conflict is unique, and every conflict resolution process must be tailored to the individuals and context of the situation. There is, however, a framework that can help you organize and then tailor the process. Following is a list of eight steps you can use to develop a conflict resolution process appropriate to the people and circumstances involved. The eight steps are fully explained in the remainder of this chapter.

Step 1: Identify the Conflict

Step 2: Decide Whether to Intervene

Step 3: Identify Parties, Issues, and Emotions

Step 4: Analyze the Conflict

Step 5: Design the Process

Step 6: Educate Parties and Get Agreement to Participate

Step 7: Conduct the Process

Step 8: Celebrate and Check In

A Watchful Eye to Sea and Sky
Step 1: Identify the Conflict

In Step 1, you learn to watch for signs of serious conflict. You can watch for changes in communication, recurring tensions, or other patterns.

page 46

A Squall Is Spied
Step 2: Decide Whether to Intervene

In Step 2, you decide whether you should help with the conflict and consider possible consequences if you do—or do not—become involved.

page 47

East Wind or West Wind?
Step 3: Identify Parties, Issues, and Emotions

In Step 3, you collect as much information about the conflict as you can, gathering each person's perspective on the issue.

page 50

Take Your Bearings
Step 4: Analyze the Conflict

In Step 4, you take time to formally analyze the conflict based on your information gathering.

page 53

Head into the Waves
Step 5: Design the Process

In Step 5, you plan the way in which you'll bring the parties together to address the conflict.

page 65

All Hands on Deck!
Step 6: Educate Parties and Get Agreement to Participate

In Step 6, you explain everything that will happen in the conflict resolution process and ask each person to agree to participate.

page 73

Into the Gale!
Step 7: Conduct the Process

In Step 7, you hold one or more meetings to help the parties find a creative solution to their differences.

page 75

Shore Leave!
Step 8: Celebrate and Check In

In Step 8, you celebrate and set up a system to be sure the agreement is followed and the parties are satisfied.

page 79

A Watchful Eye to Sea and Sky
Step 1: Identify the Conflict

When not plotting courses and checking in with the crew, the ship's captain can be seen above deck, watchful eye to the sea and sky. Though it's important to study the skies for signs of troubled weather, most times storms will find you. Still, there is a much greater benefit to finding trouble before it finds you. Usually conflicts identified early are easier to resolve because they have not escalated to a high level of emotional intensity or complexity. By the time people are uncomfortable enough to bring a conflict to your attention, the turbulence has been brewing for some time. People will have invested a great deal of emotion, thought, and energy in the conflict. Their assumptions about the other party will have multiplied, other incidents will have been added to the original one, and feelings will be more intense and negative.

You need all your senses to take note of possible storms brewing. As difficult as it is to find time in your busy schedule, make some time to simply focus on the people in your workplace. Set a time to watch your staff, listen to them, and get a feel for their tone, demeanor, and body language. Do this during a staff meeting, over lunch, and at the coffee pot; it is more a matter of focus than of actually performing a new activity. Look for changes in behavior or patterns of communication. Because conflict is uncomfortable for most people, you will see them reacting to one another differently when they are in conflict. Here are some cues to look for:

Silence. A drop in the amount of communication can often be a signal that something is going on. Conflict is one possibility.

Eye contact. Watch for a change in how people make eye contact. People of European heritage will often avoid eye contact with an individual with whom they are in conflict. (As this is a culturally specific behavior, be aware of cultural differences when interpreting eye contact.)

Humor. Note changes in the level of humor and laughter in interactions. Note whether the nature of the humor changes, particularly if it becomes sarcastic or cynical.

Word choice. Listen for euphemisms for conflict. Listen for epithets that describe alienation of individuals in the work group.

Tone of voice. Pay attention to intonation as words are spoken—particularly changes that might indicate a conflict is occurring. (Note that intonation varies with culture and to some degree with gender, so you need to know the sounds of your staff well before rushing to judgment.)

Body language. Watch how people position their bodies during interactions. Remember that some body language is culturally specific. However, the activity of mirroring positions and movements (matching another person's gestures) is shared as a signal of harmony in almost all cultures.

Change in social patterns. Be aware if social patterns change noticeably—for example, a change in who goes to lunch or social events together and who is excluded. Such changes can indicate conflict.

Style differences. Look for significant differences among individuals in their work and decision-making styles. Unless staff members have learned to recognize and value different styles, these can be a common source—or sign—of conflict.

Recurring problems. Recurring troubles between specific individuals or the same staff positions even when filled by different people may indicate system-induced conflicts.

Cross-program tensions. Watch for recurring tensions between programs or administrative parts of the organization. Some tensions are built into organizational systems as checks and balances, but some go beyond the check and balance function and become dysfunctional. They may be the unintentional result of an outmoded or useless organizational system.

Using all your many senses and skills, you may have identified a conflict. Now you have to decide what to do about it. The next section will help you do that.

A Squall Is Spied
Step 2: Decide Whether to Intervene

If you think intervention in a particular conflict is needed, consider the following questions.

1. Are you the most appropriate person to help resolve this conflict?
2. Can you (or whoever you identify) be objective about the people and issues?
3. What are the likely consequences of not resolving this issue at this point?
4. Can you make the time to deal with the resolution process?

1. Are you the most appropriate person to help resolve this conflict?

If your organization has managers with conflict resolution skills, they may be just the help you need. (This is a good argument for developing conflict resolution skills in your managers and supervisors—and ultimately in your whole staff and board.) Decide whether one of these managers is more appropriate to intervene in this particular conflict. This is especially advisable if the conflict is between people for whom a particular manager is responsible; you don't want to undermine the man-ager's credibility among staff by unwarranted interference. However, each conflict situation has to be assessed on its own merits, considering manager's objectivity, conflict resolution skills, the people involved, and the situation itself. Having conflicts managed by leaders who are not at the top of the organizational ladder has its benefits. Parties do not wonder if their issue is "even bigger than they thought" as they would if the executive or board chair gets involved. Also, if a dispute is not satisfactorily resolved by a lower level of management, it can then be considered by a higher level, which allows time and additional expertise to be brought to bear before the dispute either goes to the organization's board or to an external or more formal conflict resolution process.

Though an organization's board of directors is its last resort for internal conflict resolution, be aware that boards themselves are often unskilled in conflict management and are frequently averse to conflict. When a conflict comes to a board for resolution, there is frequently a sense that management did not handle the conflict well (even though this may not be true). There is also a potential for uninformed board members to take sides between staff members, creating a new conflict at the board level.

Though the general rule is to handle conflicts as far down on the organizational ladder as possible, conflict between managers or between supervisors and their employees may need executive intervention. Unique circumstances may require you to handle conflicts throughout the organization.

Once you have decided whether you are the most appropriate person to help resolve the conflict, you can begin to answer question 2.

2. Can you (or whoever you identify) be objective about the people and issues?

From our histories together, our personal styles, and a myriad of other factors, all of us have opinions and feelings about the people with whom we work. If you have strong feelings or preferences about any of the parties in a dispute, it will be difficult for you to be objective. In the midst of the process, it will be nearly impossible to mask your personal preferences about people. If these preferences are known, you won't be viewed as neutral by any of the parties. Be brutally honest with yourself. In regard to the parties in the conflict, you must be able to wholeheartedly say to yourself that you can be objective and impartial. If you find objectivity a challenge, seek another person to help manage this conflict.

In regard to the issues, however, you really are not neutral. You are an advocate for the well-being of the organization you lead. This does not mean you propose your preferred solution to the conflict or adhere blindly to the status quo, but if a proposed solution is bad for the organization (for example, if it breaks an important existing policy or sets a precedent that will create problems), you should help the disputants find solutions that work for them and the organization.

Don't rush to put out fire

It is good to be alert to the symptoms of conflict, but you don't need to step in immediately to resolve every conflict you see. Many conflicts resolve themselves over time. Misunderstandings are clarified, the relative importance of an issue in conflict decreases, or the issue itself changes. Remember, conflict is neutral and it can serve as a stimulant to creativity and change. If individuals in the organization have the tools to deal with conflict constructively, you may see positive outcomes.

It is worthwhile to let a newly developing conflict play out a little before intervening, especially if the parties' emotions are in check and other people and activities are unaffected. However, if you see flaring tempers or sense a rising tide of interpersonal or cross-program conflict that seems to swell whenever a new issue is present, you will need to decide on an intervention. Such conflicts are worth looking into because they will not resolve themselves readily and will fester until they infect others. Ongoing conflicts have the ability to change the overall climate of your organization in ways that can damage both morale and productivity.

The bottom line is this: If you feel you cannot be truly open-minded about the people or issues involved in the dispute, have others handle it. Once you have considered this question, you should also consider Question 3.

3. What are the likely consequences of not resolving this issue at this point?

Remember BATNA and WATNA? These acronyms help a person think through the consequences of entering into or breaking off a conflict resolution process. BATNA, Best Alternative To a Negotiated Agreement, answers the question "What will be the best possible outcome, if this conflict is not resolved at this point." As you might guess, WATNA is the converse. It stands for the Worst Alternative To a Negotiated Agreement and looks at the "worst possible outcomes if this conflict is not resolved at this point."

BATNAs and WATNAs have two uses in assessing a conflict. First, thinking through the best and worst case outcomes for you and your organization helps you clarify how important it is to intervene and what the consequences of not doing so might be. Second, once you have determined your BATNA and WATNA, you can decide whether the time is right to intervene and whether you are willing to commit the required time and energy, which is the focus of Question 4.

4. Can you make the time to deal with the resolution process?

Conflict resolution takes time because it is predominantly a communication process. It takes the long cut, clarifying the shortcuts in communication that often contribute to misunderstandings and conflicts. It takes time to gather information about the situation, tailor a process, brief parties about the process, and conduct the conflict resolution discussions. Once you begin, you have to be prepared to efficiently but sensitively carry the process to its end. (On a positive note, the process often takes considerably less time than you imagine when, with that sinking feeling in your gut, you first see a conflict surface.)

Of course time varies based on the people and issues, but here is the time investment for an average conflict:

Figure 4. Typical time for conflict resolution	
Task	**Time required**
Hold initial conversations with parties to gather information	45-60 minutes for each person
Analyze the conflict and tailor the process	30-60 minutes
Brief parties about the process	30-45 minutes each
Conduct conflict resolution meeting(s)	60-120 minutes each

As you can see, the preliminary work you do to gather information, analyze the conflict, tailor the process, and prepare parties for the conflict resolution meeting can take longer than the meeting itself. However, the preliminary work improves the chances for successful conflict resolution.

Many conflicts are resolved in meetings of two hours or less. In cases with multiple issues, many parties, or extremely high emotions, additional meetings may be needed. However, you can use the chart above to roughly estimate how much time the process will take.

Once you have decided that you should intervene in the conflict, it is time to better understand the conflict you're faced with.

East Wind or West Wind?
Step 3: Identify Parties, Issues, and Emotions

Having spied the coming storm and decided to head into it, the wise captain takes time to size up the skies and winds. To understand a conflict well enough to determine how to facilitate a resolution process, you, like the ship's captain, need information. Start with the people who have identified themselves or whom you have identified as the parties in conflict. (It's not uncommon to find additional parties to a conflict as you talk with the identified parties.)

Following are questions you'll need to answer as you identify the people, issues, and emotions in the conflict.

1. Which people have a stake in the conflict? These are the parties.
2. Do certain groups have the same interests and positions? Think of like-minded groups as one party when you analyze the conflict.
3. How does each person see the issues (substantive, procedural, relationship, and identity) in the conflict? These are their positions and interests. Mentally note the assumptions or motives each person ascribes to others.
4. What does each party seek as a solution to the conflict? These are their positions.
5. How emotional are the people regarding the conflict?

Your first step in collecting information is simply to make note of the known parties and make appointments with them to collect information about who is involved, the issues at hand, and their feelings about the situation. As you meet with the parties, the names of other individuals may also crop up. Add these to the list of people to contact.

After you speak with each person, jot down the key answers to the five preceding questions—the parties involved, their assessment of the issues, their assumptions about each other, their desired solutions, and their emotional states. You do not need extensive notes, just something to jog your memory of the conversation when you analyze the situation. (Keep these notes in a secure place. I generally dispose of them after the conflict resolution process is complete.)

You may not need to ask for much information about the conflict to get answers to your questions. People are often so relieved to have someone who will listen to their side of the conflict that they are very forthcoming. As a result, they will tell you a great deal without your asking specific questions. However, information gathering is an art. You will receive a lot of information at once, and you must sort out the underlying issues and the emotional content that surrounds them.

Underlying issues

People frequently describe a conflict in terms of the absence of the solution they would like to see. They are also likely to describe the other party as somehow blocking that solution. In such cases, ask them to describe the parts of the problem their solution addresses. This can get you to people's underlying concerns or needs (called interests).

For example, a statement often heard in nonprofit organizations is "If we had the funding, we would offer this needed service." Lack of funding is stated as the problem. In actuality, funding is only one solution to the problem of wanting to set up a new program that requires resources. There are other solutions, but to figure them out one needs to explore the underlying needs and concerns that the stated solution of "funding" really addresses. If staff time is the underlying need funding will meet, then additional staff, volunteer staff, interns, pro bono workers, or staff reassignments are all alternative solutions to the problem of lack of funding.

Collecting information

There are two important things to remember when you start gathering information. First is to go slow. Second is that the minute you start gathering information, you are facilitating a conflict resolution process, even if you ultimately determine that another person will facilitate. Your tone at this initial step will strongly influence the tone of the whole process.

Go slow

Most Americans see a problem and want to solve it quickly. In conflict management, it is important to slow down. When collecting information, do that and only that. If you skip ahead to possible solutions, you are likely to miss important information that will cause problems later. Typically, your research will show you that information is missing or that other people need to be involved in the process. So take your time and try to get a complete version of each person's story during this step.

Information collection is facilitation

When you begin talking to parties to collect information, you have officially embarked on the conflict resolution process. Make sure that you are always perceived as impartial and that you hold information confidential (except in the special cases discussed in Chapter Four). Avoid making judgmental statements. Avoid seeming to assign blame or convey guilt. Be calm, reassuring, and optimistic. Your manner will set a long-lasting tone for future discussions. You will also be establishing a rapport important later in the process.

The exploration of what needs or concerns a proposed solution (called a position) addresses is called uncovering the interests. You will remember that interests are "the underlying needs or compelling issues of each party in a dispute." Interests often go unstated. The key interests are the essential needs and concerns that a mutually acceptable resolution must address. Understanding them is a critical part of designing a process and crafting a resolution. Sometimes it is easier for a conflict manager to recognize an interest than it is for the party holding the interest because they are so hooked into their position.

Many times people become so attached to their solutions that they lose sight of their own basic interests. Helping people articulate and understand their own interests is an important service a conflict manager offers. As part of the process of understanding positions and interests, a manager can frame the issue in a new way. (You will learn more about the technique of reframing in Chapter Three.)

Uncovering interests is actually very simple. You must learn the reasons why a person takes a particular position or suggests a particular solution. When someone in conflict proposes a solution or position, ask them to clarify why a particular solution works for them. The way you get to why is important. A direct why can make people feel that you doubt their reasoning, which can make them defensive. Avoid a tone of voice or phrasing that sounds interrogating. Rather, approach the question in a conversational manner. Sometimes you can state, as a guess, what you think a party's interest might be and check it out with them. If you guessed right, great. If you guessed wrong, they will correct you. You both win either way. An added benefit of this process is that when parties say or hear their interests articulated, they feel understood. They also discover what elements a resolution must contain to satisfy them. (You will learn more about the technique of restating in Chapter Three of this book.)

Emotional content

As you uncover the issues and interests in a conflict, you will also encounter the emotions that surround it. Many people have strong feelings when they are engaged in a conflict; adults often experience a conflict with the same emotional intensity they felt as children. People may describe their feelings as they talk with you, but you are even more likely to sense their feelings through their facial expressions, intonation, and body language. They will express—and you will observe—anger, hurt, sadness, guilt, defensiveness, and many other feelings in any combination. It is important to acknowledge these feelings, but you must remember that you are not responsible for changing their feelings. However, your recognition of an individual's feelings will usually lower the intensity of the feeling.

Whatever you say, be sincere; it is better not to say anything than to use "canned" statements like "what I think I hear you saying is_____ ." Such phrases are overused and feel manipulative to the person who hears them. Use only affirming comments that feel natural and sincere to you. This makes them believable. Some examples include:

- "You seem very upset about that."
- "Does _____ make you angry?"
  (Use when you think you see nonverbal signs of anger.)
- "Are you worried about _____?"
- "So when that happened, you felt _____?"

Affirming comments are frequently offered in the form of questions. This enables the party to either confirm or correct what you think they may be feeling. Many people have a limited vocabulary for naming feelings, so it might be helpful to use a variety of words that describe emotion. Here are some words that identify common feelings people have during conflict: happy, sad, frustrated, cheated, satisfied, proud, embarrassed, belittled, relieved, exhausted, used, worried, frightened, ashamed, guilty, sympathetic, upset, understood, anxious, humiliated, misunderstood, elated, and concerned—to name just a few! (You will learn more about affirming statements in Chapter Three.)

Many of us shy away from talking about feelings when we think another person is emotional. We worry that talking about feelings will unleash a flood of emotion neither we nor they can handle. This rarely happens and when it does, it often relieves the pressure and helps the person manage their emotions better. More commonly, identifying feelings generally has the effect of lowering people's levels of emotion. Naming emotions also conveys empathy.

If someone's emotions do overwhelm them, just be patient and wait them out. Offer time, company, or privacy, as they wish, and possibly a tissue or drink of water. The strong emotions will pass, and the pressure of restraining pent-up emotions will be relieved. Then the person will be able to discuss the issue in a more lucid manner.

Take Your Bearings
Step 4: Analyze the Conflict

On the open sea, captains of old used a compass and sextant to get their bearings. Getting your bearings on the currents of conflict requires tools of another sort—your analytic abilities, managerial judgment, and some creative thinking. You'll screen for problems such as harassment, maltreatment, or illegal behavior, which should be dealt with in processes other than this. You'll sort the people you've identified into parties and try to understand what their positions are. You'll discover if you need to gather more information before proceeding. You will apply all of these tools to the information you gathered to chart a course to help people resolve their conflict.

Your analysis will answer the following questions:

1. Can this conflict be handled by this informal process?
2. Who are all the people with stakes in this conflict?
3. Are these individuals capable of making rational, informed decisions?
4. What are the power relationships among the individuals?
5. What gender or cultural differences need to be considered?

6. How does each person describe the overall conflict?

7. What are each party's positions? (What solutions do they seek?)

8. What does each party say—or what can be inferred—about their key needs and concerns (their interests)?

9. What assumptions are people making about one another?

10. Do some individuals share interests and positions?

11. Are people's interests substantive, procedural, relationship-based, or identity-based? Which of these is the primary concern?

12. Is the conflict interpersonal or is it induced by the system—or is it both?

13. Are there known limitations to potential resolutions that you must impose on behalf of the organization?

To help you organize these questions, I've provided three worksheets in the appendix. (See Appendix B, Worksheets.) At the end of this section, I've provided a case study showing how I used these worksheets to analyze a conflict I was asked to mediate.

1. Can this conflict be handled by this informal process?

The first step is to screen the conflict to decide whether it requires a conflict resolution process different from the one described. Such situations include

- Harassment (page 127)
- Discrimination (page 133)
- The involvement of vulnerable adults or children (page 136)
- Evidence of illegal behavior (page 137)
- Actions covered under union grievance procedures (page 126)

All of these situations require special processes that may make them inappropriate for the informal conflict management process suggested in this book. If you find these situations as you gather information, you will need to follow the particular processes designed for them. The first step is to review your organization's personnel policies so you understand the organization's established procedures and policies. If your nonprofit is unionized, reviewing the contract and grievance procedures is your next step. Chapter Four discusses these and other unique conflicts. Seek advisers with expertise in these situations.

2. Who are all the people with stakes in this conflict?

In Step 3, you identified the people, the parties, their issues, and the emotions surrounding the conflict. Now is the time to revisit the list to be sure you know the name of every person who is substantively affecting or being affected by the conflict. These are the people to involve in the conflict management process. You may discover more (or different) parties than originally expected. If you find new parties in the middle of the process, they need to be brought into the discussion—and that means backing up the process a bit so the new parties can catch up.

In addition to the people who are parties to the conflict, there are others who may be directly affected by or concerned about the ultimate resolution. List these people and your supposition about their potential interests. Though these people probably won't be included in the conflict resolution meetings, you may need to ask for their expert advice or opinion as options are being devised.

3. Are these individuals capable of making rational, informed decisions?

After you have named all the individuals, you need to decide whether they are competent to participate in a conflict resolution process. Most people are. For example, a person who seems overwrought with emotion is still capable of participating; a person who seems overwrought with emotion and is acting out violently is not.

Nonprofits that work with mentally handicapped individuals or other vulnerable people may need to follow a different process when a conflict affects them. In situations in which people are mentally handicapped, one solution is to have a trusted and competent adviser work with the party throughout the process. If you determine that even with such help the person cannot participate in the process, you might consider whether a proxy might work (with the person's or their guardian's permission). A proxy is a person whose role is much like that of an international diplomat. When conducted with a proxy, the conflict resolution process works a lot like shuttle diplomacy. It entails a lot of conferring and very clear communications between the proxy and the party. If these options are not viable, then it may be unwise to continue an informal conflict management process. (For information on conflicts involving maltreatment of vulnerable people, see Chapter Four.)

If you decide that some individuals are not capable of participating, then the informal conflict resolution process is not appropriate. You will need to involve people outside your organization and use a different process.

What makes the process likely to succeed?

Resolving conflict through an informal process is more promising if certain characteristics are present. If the conflict you are managing has only a few of these characteristics, you may still ultimately decide that an informal process is the best. Here are the characteristics that make informal conflict resolution most promising.

- The people involved are uncomfortable enough with the dispute to want to end it

- There are significant costs or other disincentives to continuing the dispute

- The parties have done equal harm

- The people involved have had a history of positive interactions

- The people involved will relate to one another again in the future

- The people involved have the authority to settle their dispute

- The parties display empathy for one another

- The issues are substantive or procedural, rather than values-driven

- The parties are skilled communicators

- Emotions are not too high

- The stakes are small and a settlement seems probable

- The conflict manager is trusted by the parties

4. What are the power relationships among the individuals?

Having identified the parties and decided they are competent to participate, you must then analyze the power relationships among them. If necessary, return to the section, Power and Conflict (pages 34-37), which describes types of power. You need to consider two things about power. The first is to determine who has what sorts of power, and who accedes (or does not accede) to that power. The second is to think about how the parties have used their power in the conflict thus far. When one party's use of power is perceived as forcing or blocking, it often creates relationship issues where none existed. If it's helpful, record the type of power an individual has on the worksheet on page 162.

In the next section, Step 5: Design the Process, you will plan how to balance power during the conflict resolution. For now, all you need to do is note the types of power involved and how they have been used.

5. What gender or cultural differences need to be considered?

Now you will apply the information you learned in Chapter One about how culture and gender influence communications and activities in the workplace. Might culture, gender, or other communication differences have created misunderstandings? Are there misunderstandings based on stereotypes regarding culture or gender? Consider these and note your thoughts on the worksheets. You will use this information when you get to Step 5: Design the Process.

6. How does each person describe the overall conflict?

This question gets at what each person says the overall conflict is about. Use this information to assess how the parties place blame or claim responsibility in the conflict. Then consider how readily the parties might agree to participate in a conflict resolution process.

7. What are each party's positions? (What solutions do they seek?)

As explained in Chapter One, a party's position is the solution they propose to resolve the conflict—usually, a solution that addresses their interests only. Note that when stating their overview of the conflict, parties often state their positions as the lack of something.

8. What does each party say—or what can be inferred—about their key needs and concerns (their interests)?

Understanding each party's interests gives you a picture of the content of the conflict and even shows you possibilities for resolution. You may have to infer a party's interests from what they have told you in your information-gathering conversations. If you have done this, it will be essential in the conflict management meetings to ask if your inferences are correct. But for the purpose of analyzing a conflict, you can start with educated guesses regarding a party's interests. Be sure to note which interests the party identified and which you inferred.

9. What assumptions are people making about one another?

In Chapter One you learned about cognitive dissonance, our mental practice of "filling in the blanks" or changing our perceptions, when new information does not jibe with our current reality. Often the assumptions people in conflict make are the result of the cognitive dissonance they experience. Understanding these assumptions will give you important clues about issues that need to be discussed at the conflict resolution meeting. The ultimate goal is that all parties have the same information. This significantly increases the likelihood of a resolution. Because parties in conflict make many negative assumptions about each other, dispelling inaccurate assumptions is a major contribution to mending relationships. However, in the analysis phase, noting these assumptions is all you need do.

10. Do some individuals share interests and positions?

In Step 3, you gathered information about the people, their positions and interests, their emotions, and their power. Now is the time to group these individuals into parties. Make rough groupings based on the similarities in their interests and positions. You may need to adjust these groupings as you further analyze the various interests of the people involved. People with similar positions, even if their interests differ, are likely to view one another as allies. When they discover that their interests differ, they may dissolve their alliance.

11. Are people's interests substantive, procedural, relationship-based, or identity-based? Which of these is the primary concern?

As each party's interests and positions come to light, it is helpful to consider whether they are about relationships among people, substantive matters (resources or time), processes and procedures (how decisions are made or how systems work), or strongly held self-identifying beliefs or practices. Most conflicts contain more than one of these types of interests, but it is helpful to sort them out when possible. Knowing the types of interests underlying the conflict will help you think about the goals of the process you will design in subsequent steps. Finally, you may note which interests seem to be most important to the parties. These are likely the key matters that must be addressed to get a mutually satisfactory resolution.

12. Is the conflict interpersonal or is it induced by the system— or is it both?

Sorting out whether a conflict is interpersonal or system-induced is challenging because conflicts initially created by organizational systems frequently become personal. Consider whether there are procedures, policies, or practices in the organization that are unnecessarily fostering conflict. Be aware that some systems that create conflict in organizations are necessary: they are designed as checks and balances that preserve accountability and distribute power. Other system-induced conflicts are vestiges of policies, procedures, or decisions that are no longer needed. As you analyze a conflict, be alert to system-induced conflicts and be open-minded about changing the organizational systems that create them unnecessarily. Such conflicts may lead to positive changes in your organization's policies or procedures.

13. Are there known limitations to potential resolutions that you must impose on behalf of the organization?

As much as you care about the individuals involved in your nonprofit, your first responsibility is to the organization you lead. You may find that some potential solutions to conflict are limited by finances, policies, mission goals, ethical standards, union procedures, or legal requirements.

For example, a nonprofit neighborhood day care center wrestled with a conflict between its mission and a potential new funding source. A contribution from a huge corporation to an umbrella agency made new grants possible that would help the day care center meet rigorous accreditation standards and improve its quality.

Know your limits

Generating solutions without regard to existing organizational limitations can raise unrealistic expectations, waste time and effort, and create disillusionment when parties learn their solutions are not feasible. You will lose considerable credibility if limits are sprung on parties toward the end of the process. You may not always be able to identify every limitation as you analyze the conflict and design the process. Identify those you can; as others come to light, alert the parties and explain the limitations and why they exist.

The neighborhood day care center applied for and received a grant. The grant contract was sent to the board president for his signature. Upon reading the contract, the president noted that by accepting the award, employees of the funding corporation would, in perpetuity, receive priority for their children to attend the day care center. This was against the mission of the organization, which was established to serve an economically and racially diverse clientele from the neighborhood. Accepting the grant would require the day care to serve the children of the corporation before those of the neighborhood.

The board was in conflict over whether to accept the much needed money. It had to weigh whether its mission of service to the neighborhood was more important than the financial support, which would improve its quality. The board resolved the conflict by declining the grant, and the people most concerned about maintaining the focus on diversity and neighborhood agreed to head an alternative fundraising effort to pay for accreditation and improved quality.

As much as possible be aware of these limitations in advance of a conflict and help the parties understand the constraints on their solutions. In doing this, first be sure that the organization's limits are indeed nonnegotiable. Then be prepared to explain why the limits are necessary for the sake of the organization. You will probably not use this information immediately, but it is wise to have thought it through during the conflict analysis—before embarking on the conflict management process.

The kind of formal analysis I've just described is not natural for most of us. To help you see how it works, the following example shows how I used this process to analyze a conflict. Blank copies of the worksheets that follow can be found in Appendix B, Worksheets.

The scene

I was asked to facilitate a mediation between two employees of a nonprofit human services organization who came from different ethnic and racial backgrounds. Susan and Crystal, both excellent social workers, had been making home visits as a team for about two years. Their conflicts were about coordination of efforts, time management, and different styles of communication. In addition, Crystal, an American Indian, felt that Susan, who was Jewish, was disrespectful of American Indian cultural heritage and observances. Similarly, Susan felt that Crystal lacked respect for her Jewish heritage and customs. This was presented as the key issue between them. In addition to Susan and Crystal, other people with an interest in the conflict included Neal, the director of the nonprofit social service agency for which the team worked (and their immediate supervisor); Leah, a friend of Susan; and Roger, a friend of Crystal.

The sample worksheets that follow on pages 60–64 show how I analyzed the conflict. Typically, I fill out a new copy of Worksheet 1 for each individual in the conflict, and then transfer the information to the grid in Worksheet 2, which combines the information collected on each person in Worksheet 1. For the sake of brevity, my example shows only Worksheet 1 for Susan. The information on the other individuals is summarized on Worksheet 2.

WORKSHEET 1   Conflict Analysis–Individuals

Fill out this worksheet for each person involved in the conflict.

Name: **Susan**

Expressed Positions

> **Wants Crystal to come to appointments on time**
> **Wants Crystal to respect her ethnic/religious background**
> **Wants Crystal to stop criticizing her professionalism**

Expressed Interests (mar k key interests)

- ✓ **Wants to be able to depend on coworker**
- ✓ **Wants her professional skills recognized and valued**
- ✓ **Wants respect for her identity (ethnic/religious)**

Interests you inf erred (mar k key interests)

- ✓ **Uncomfortable with conflict; wants it to end**
- ✓ **Wants to reestablish previous friendship with Crystal**
- ✓ **Wants to keep her job**

Gender, cultural, and racial diff erences to consider

> **East coast raised/European tradition/Jewish/female**

Emotional state

> **Hurt, fearful, and angry—all emotions under control**

Power

a) Types of power a vailable

> **Informal power with peers; informal power as a longtime employee; nuisance power**

b) How has this per son used power in the conflict

- **Informal power—has spread negative comments among staff**
- **Nuisance power—has complained frequently to get Executive Director involved**

How does this per son describe the conflict?

- **Coworker does not show up for appointments or shows up late**
- **Coworker criticizes her professionalism**
- **Coworker makes slurs about Jews**
- **Executive Director says he may fire her if she can't work with coworker**

What assumptions is this per son making about others in the conflict?

- **Coworker is anti-Semitic**
- **Coworker is undependable; doesn't take work seriously**
- **Coworker uses unprofessional, unorthodox methods**
- **Executive Director is shirking his responsibility of dealing with coworker performance**
- **Coworker should leave her ethnicity out of her work**

WORKSHEET 2   Conflict Analysis–The Parties and Their Interests

Group the individuals you listed in Worksheet 1 into parties with similar positions and interests. Note their positions, interests, power relationships, and emotional states.

Party 1: Susan

Position	Interest	Power	Emotional State
Wants Crystal to come to appointments on time Wants Crystal to respect her ethnic/ religious background Wants Crystal to stop criticizing her professionalism	Wants to be able to depend on coworker Wants respect for her identity (Jewish) Wants her professional skills recognized and valued Wants to reestablish previous friendship	Informal	Hurt, fearful, angry; under control

Party 2: Crystal

Position	Interest	Power	Emotional State
Wants Susan to respect her culture Wants Susan to treat Indian clients appropriately Wants Susan to stop telling her what to do Wants to stop fighting	Wants her American Indian identity respected Wants her knowledge of American Indian culture respected and applied when working with American Indian clients Wants more flexibility in scheduling; wants equitable power relationship Wants to end dispute; wants to return to friendly relations	Informal	Angry, hurt; under control

(continued)

Worksheet 2   Conflict Analysis–The   Parties and Their Interests

Now list those people indirectly concerned with the conflict.

Concerned Person: **Neal**

Position	Interest	Power	Emotional State
Sick of the conflict; does not want to spend more time on it Will fire one or both parties if they can't work together	Wants employees focused on job Wants the conflict to end because it is creating morale problems in organization	Formal--he's their executive and supervisor	Exasperated

Concerned Person: **Leah**

Position	Interest	Power	Emotional State
Wants to help and support her friend	Wants to provide solidarity for Susan's Jewish identity	Associational; has referred clients to organization	Concerned

Concerned Person: **Roger**

Position	Interest	Power	Emotional State
Wants to provide advice and support for Crystal	Crystal is member of his tribal band; wants to support her and needs her community interaction	Formal, but outside organization --is a community leader	Supportive

(continued)

Worksheet 2   Conflict Analysis–The Parties and Their Interests

Finally, list all the interests identified by all people grouped by parties (if possible). Note if these interests are substantive, procedural, relationship-based, or identity-based. Mark their key interests.

Interests–Party 1: Susan	substantive	procedural	relationship-based	identity-based
Wants to be able to depend on coworker		✓		
Wants her professional skills recognized and valued				✓
Wants respect for her identity				✓
Wants to reestablish friendship			✓	
Uncomfortable with conflict; wants it to end			✓	
(Leah) Support for Jewish identity				✓

Interests–Party 2: Crystal	substantive	procedural	relationship-based	identity-based
Wants to end dispute			✓	
Wants more flexibility in scheduling appointments		✓		
Wants her knowledge of American Indian culture respected and applied when working with American Indian clients		✓		✓
Wants to return to friendly relations			✓	
Wants her American Indian identity respected				✓
(Roger) Wants to provide advice to and support for a member of his tribal band			✓	✓

Interests–Party 3: Neal	substantive	procedural	relationship-based	identity-based
Wants employees focused on job		✓		
Wants the conflict to end because it is creating morale problems in organization		✓	✓	

WORKSHEET 3   Conflict Analysis–Overall Analysis

First, review the checklist for screening whether a conflict is appropriate for informal conflict resolution processes.

1. Are there allegations of harassment or abuse? (If answer is yes—use other established processes.)

   No, but this has the potential for escalating to harassment; keep alert.

2. Is there evidence of criminal activity? (If answer is yes, consult attorney to determine action to take—in some cases, conflict resolution processes are still appropriate.)

   No

3. Are vulnerable persons involved (children, elderly, mentally retarded, mentally ill, etc.)? (If so, consider whether appropriate support and process design will facilitate an informal conflict resolution process.)

   No, but because this team routinely conducts home visits and one is complaining about the professionalism of the other, their conflict could affect some vulnerable parties—the children they see. Keep alert.

Second, review the characteristics of the conflict.

4. Is there a union contract that has bearing on this conflict?

   No

5. Does the conflict seem to be interpersonal or is it induced by the system—or is it both? (Describe)

   Seems interpersonal, but if racism is involved, there may be some systemic elements. Both coworkers seem to be uncomfortable in the conflict and state that they want to go back to an earlier friendly relationship. Both seem most stung by the insensitivity of the other to identity issues important to them. Each has also spoken negatively about the other among other coworkers and this too seems to be one of the areas of hurt.

6. Does the conflict seem to take any of the classic shapes as discussed in Chapter One on pages 18-20? These shapes—direct conflict, spiral conflict, subtle conflict, and violent conflict—may give you clues to yet unidentified issues.

   Conflict looks direct—parties are talking about substantive, relationship, and identity issues. Seems to have been escalating over an eight-month period.

7. Are there currently known limitations to potential resolutions that you must impose on behalf of the organization?

   No

8. Who is the most appropriate person to facilitate the conflict resolution process?

   Conflict manager external to the organization. The executive seems to be washing hands of the conflict—he's using threats to try to change employee behavior and seems emotionally entangled (exasperated) by the conflict.

Head into the Waves
Step 5: Design the Process

In high seas it's best to head into the waves, where they can break safely over the bow. In the same way, it's best to steer your nonprofit headlong into the waves of conflict. In Step 5, having finished your analysis of the situation, you'll plot your course for the conflict resolution process.

It is possible that after you've concluded your analysis of the conflict in Step 4, you'll realize that you are not the best person to manage this particular conflict. Relax—all is not lost! Review the material on pages 47-50 in Step 2: Decide Whether to Intervene. Keep these thoughts
in mind as you mull over possible candidates for the job:

- The person must have conflict management skills.

- All parties must view the person as impartial.

- You will need to talk with the person about the information you have gathered—you can't just turn over your worksheets to him or her.

- The person will need to be the one to design the process (this step), with your advice.

- You will need to tell the person of any restrictions to possible solutions you identified in your analysis.

- The person will need to check back with you if proposed solutions have implications for other organizational policies and procedures.

- You will need to inform the parties with whom you spoke during the information-gathering phase. They will probably want to know why you have selected this person as conflict manager, that the person has your confidence, and what strengths he or she will bring to the process. The new conflict manager may want to meet briefly with each party to develop rapport.

- Most importantly, the person you select as conflict manager needs to know that they have your backing, support, and trust.

An external mediator will have their own ideas about process. Be sure to select a mediator who is flexible and sensitive to your organization's culture.

If you or an internal conflict manager will be designing the process, continue to follow the steps in this book. Though you (or the person you've selected as the internal conflict manager) will tailor the process to the situation at hand, keep in mind that most conflict management processes share these common sequential phases:

Choosing a mediator from outside the organization

If no one in the organization can be a impartial conflict manager, find a mediator. Nonprofit community mediation organizations offer low-cost or free services using trained volunteers and professionals. In many states the supreme court or attorney general's offices can suggest professional mediators, as can local chapters of professional associations like the Society of Professionals in Conflict Resolution, the American Arbitration Association, or the National Association of Community Mediators. Individual mediators are often listed in the commercial pages of the telephone directory. Word-of-mouth is also an excellent source. Chapter Four (pages 139-142) has information about getting external help. Refer to it before interviewing external mediators.

- An exploratory period in which you get a general sense of the conflict, the parties involved, and the overall issues (you did this in Step 3: Identify the Parties, Issues, and Emotions). You also encourage the parties to participate in a conflict resolution process (Step 6: Educate Parties and Get Agreement to Participate).

- A differentiation phase in which people raise and you note the concerns, needs, and feelings that make up the conflict (Step 7: Conduct the Process).

- An integration phase in which these are categorized and prioritized, potential solutions are generated and evaluated, and feelings are clarified and validated (Step 7: Conduct the Process).

- A resolution phase in which parties select mutually acceptable solutions (to the parties and to the organization you represent) and mend relationships (Step 7: Conduct the Process).

Your analysis of the conflict will dictate if and how you want to approach these phases, as well as how you might want to modify the process steps outlined on pages 73-74 of Step 6: Educate Parties and Get Agreement to Participate. Following are the questions you will need to answer:

1. What are the goals of the process?
2. How much time will the process take? (An estimate)
3. How will power imbalances be handled?
4. How will you or another conflict manager handle people's emotions regarding the conflict?
5. In what setting will the meetings occur?
6. How will you or another conflict manager protect people's need for privacy and confidentiality?
7. If this is a system-induced conflict, who needs to be consulted if changes in policy or procedure are part of the resolution?

1. What are the goals of the process?

All right, let's state the obvious first: The goal is to end the conflict. But there is more to it than that. Conflicts may require additional goals:

- If the people involved must work together regularly, an important goal will be to reestablish trust and harmony—to restore the relationship. If this does not occur, you will find new conflicts rekindling left and right. This situation calls for a relationship goal.

- If the conflict is with a vendor who you will likely quit using and with whom a lawsuit would be very costly, resolving the substantive interests is much more important than resolving the relationship issues. (There are always some of each, but they vary in significance.) This situation calls for a substantive goal.

- If the conflict is between management and employees or management and the board of directors, the goal might include changing or clarifying processes in the organization along with rebuilding damaged relationships. Here procedural interests are foremost, coupled with relationship interests when staff and board will continue to work together. This situation calls for a procedural goal.

Identifying the key goals of the process will help you decide how much effort and time to invest on certain issues, which in turn is likely to shape the way you facilitate conflict management meetings. As you design the conflict resolution process, take a moment to state the goals for relationship, substantive, procedural, and other issues. Look over the most important interests on the conflict analysis worksheet you completed in Step 4. Note the types of interests marked as key to the parties (substantive, procedural, relationship-based, or identity-based). These will point to the goals. Consider whether you think this conflict takes a classic shape. If it is shaped like a spiral or subtle conflict, anticipate that unidentified interests will arise in the resolution process. Also think about the future activities of the people involved in the conflict, because future interactions definitely influence goals. It is useful to think this through in advance, but don't be surprised if things change as you get new information in the conflict resolution meeting. Having a process in mind gives you and the parties confidence to undertake the conflict resolution, but flexibility is critical to its success.

2. How much time will the process take? (An estimate)

Figure 4 on page 49 showed the average time a conflict resolution process might take. Now that you have spoken with all the parties, you can estimate time for this particular conflict. To develop an estimate, consider the number of people involved, the quantity and complexity of issues, how close the parties are in their positions and interests, and how damaged relationships are. The conflict manager and the parties will find an estimate useful for planning their own work. Just remind everyone to be flexible—conflict resolution is a process with twists, turns, and surprises!

Used judiciously, time limitations can encourage people to settle disputes. I have held many conflict resolution meetings in the evening in public libraries. When the librarians announce that the library will close in fifteen minutes, the parties become more focused and they frequently resolve their issues as we are literally being shooed out the door. Time running out or the possibility of having to devote another meeting to the

How long should meetings last?

I don't recommend marathon meetings. Because conflict resolution is intense, meetings should last no more than two hours. After this time, the conflict manager and the parties rarely have the mental stamina to be productive. The two-hour rule creates a deadline for each meeting and gives people time to consider what has been said before meeting again. Spacing meetings is an art. People need time to contemplate between meetings, but too much time requires the group to backtrack. Of course meeting time is often dictated by participants' calendars and by the need to complete tasks such as information gathering before the next meeting.

Ways to balance power before, during, and after conflict resolution meetings

Before

- If the weaker party fears retribution from the stronger party, choose a conflict manager who has authority over the stronger party and who knows the issues; people generally try to behave reasonably and fairly in the presence of someone with authority over them.

- If you have authority over the more powerful party, that is a strong reason for you to be the conflict manager.

- Review the section on different types of power (pages 34-37); consider the powers each party has available and how these might be used to level the playing field.

- Help the weaker party understand the different types of power they have available to them such as power of expertise, association, and information.

- Assure that both parties have access to the same information regarding matters being discussed.

- Encourage the weaker party to get help understanding the information, if it is new to them (don't coach the person yourself, however, as you will jeopardize your impartiality; have a supervisor, colleague, or friend help with this).

- Encourage both parties, but especially the weaker one, to prepare thoroughly for the meetings, including rehearsing what they will say or role-playing with a friend or colleague.

- Help the parties, especially the weaker one, to explore assumptions they may hold about their options and choices (do this during the meeting as well).

(continued)

issue helps people sort out their issues and come to conclusion. Like many conflict resolution techniques, deadlines must be used like a spice—just a little, at the right moment.

Sometimes having a set time in mind helps people feel good about resolving an issue sooner than anticipated—it sets everyone up as working together to beat the clock. Any time you can get people in conflict to work together or agree—even about the weather—you are reinforcing their ability to work through a conflict together.

3. How will power imbalances be handled?

In Step 4: Analyze the Conflict, you noted the types of power each individual and party had. Now you will plan how to balance those powers. Handling gross power imbalances is tricky. Because organizations are generally hierarchical, people have different degrees of authority and power over others. Most people view such power as the only power in an organization and so find it intimidating to try to resolve conflict with someone they view as more powerful. Often their biggest fear is retribution by the more powerful individual. Fear of retribution frequently keeps people at different levels in the organization from dealing with conflict. You will need to deal with this fear up front—usually before people agree to try to resolve their conflict. For ideas about this, see the sidebar on ways to balance power before, during, and after conflict resolution meetings (pages 68-69).

To maintain trust, you must employ power-balancing techniques very subtly, using them primarily with individual parties and not in the presence of others. Efforts at balancing power are readily perceived as taking sides, which will greatly diminish your effectiveness as a conflict manager. Power imbalances should be considered while designing a conflict management process, during the conflict resolution process itself, and as resolutions are developed. Because power ebbs and flows between parties throughout a conflict management process, you will need to remain observant of power continually.

4. How will you handle people's emotions regarding the conflict?

In Step 3: Identify Parties, Issues, and Emotions, you assessed the intensity of people's emotions. Now it's time to incorporate your assessment into the design of the conflict management process.

As mentioned before, just talking about the conflict with an impartial person often considerably de-escalates emotions. But don't expect a person to remain emotionless at a face-to-face meeting with the other party just because he or she has released emotions in previous discussions with you. Like power, emotions ebb and flow, especially during the early part of a conflict resolution process when people are first airing their differences.

The intensity of people's emotions is a clue to the importance of their issues. But don't underestimate the importance of feelings, even if emotions don't seem high. Many resolutions ultimately hinge on an apology or other acknowledgment of one party's misjudgment of people or events.

Here are some guidelines for designing a process that accounts for people's emotional states and fosters a resolution that helps repair wounded feelings:

- Attend to people's need to manage their emotions by having tissues and water within reach.

- Seat people in conflict so that when they look up they are not forced to make eye contact.

- Assure that the meeting room is private, so that if people get emotional they don't have to worry that uninvolved people can hear or see them.

- Make all parties aware that they can call a break or a caucus at any time—for example, when emotions are getting difficult to manage.

- Call breaks or caucuses yourself if you sense that people are getting quite emotional.

- Be available to hold caucuses with emotional parties, so they can emote in private with you. (This is a situation in which you will want to empathize, but not sympathize.) Be sure to hold caucuses with both parties.

- Tactfully name emotions (understating them somewhat) to help people feel understood and de-escalate emotions.

With agreement from all parties, people can invite someone to attend the meeting to lend emotional support. (I strongly recommend that support people NOT be allowed

- Explore and help both parties, but especially the weaker one, determine their Best Alternative To a Negotiated Agreement (BATNA) and Worst Alternative To a Negotiated Agreement (WATNA) in the conflict (see page 9); an understanding of this is empowering.

During

- Encourage the weaker person to be assertive in expressing ideas and feelings.

- Let the weaker party tell his or her perspective first; this sets a frame of reference for the discussion.

- Provide equal time for each party to speak, limiting interruptions, stopping inappropriate language or behavior quickly, and directing parties to frame their presentations in terms of their own experiences and feelings (as opposed to blaming or speaking for the other party).

- To constrain the more powerful party, suggest that he or she communicate in a way that keeps the weaker party from feeling intimidated.

- When appropriate, reframe issues to a shared, higher level in which each party has an equal stake.

After

- To reduce the possibility of retribution, be sure that the agreement includes some form of monitoring and evaluation of the more powerful person's behavior.

How to conduct shuttle diplomacy

Shuttle diplomacy is well-known as a technique between governments, but it is equally useful in nonprofit organizations when tensions between the two parties are so high that they can't be put in the same room. In shuttle diplomacy, an intermediary—usually, you—shuttles back and forth between the disputing parties, clarifying interests, testing potential solutions, and conveying responses until enough concerns have been addressed and emotions have de-escalated to the point that the parties can meet face-to-face.

When you conduct shuttle diplomacy start with an issue that you feel will be easy to resolve. It is even possible to carefully invent one if necessary—like some aspect of the conflict resolution process itself. As you conduct shuttle diplomacy, move gradually from easier to more difficult tensions. Once people learn that they and their "adversary" can actually agree to something—no matter how small—their anxiety and emotions decrease, making face-to-face meetings easier.

Frequently, people at the beginning of a conflict are suspicious of both the process and the other party. This makes them concerned that agreeing on an individual issue (as opposed to agreeing on the issues in total) will tie their hands later. Make it clear to them that if they develop solutions to individual issues, these will be set aside until the end, at which time the whole package of settled issues will be reviewed before being agreed upon. By making solutions to individual issues tentative until the process is complete, you will help parties feel more confident about the process. The benefit of an early tentative agreement about some issue is that it sends a message to each party that the other may not be as hostile, obstreperous, or negative as they imagine.

(continued)

---

to participate in the discussions. Ground rules for outsider participation are provided on page 74.)

Use your interpersonal knowledge and intuition to judge people's emotions. If you think that emotions are so high that the parties cannot face one another without an emotional outburst, you might design the first phase of the discussion as a form of shuttle diplomacy on your part. (See the sidebar "How to conduct shuttle diplomacy" (pages 70-71) for details on how to use the technique.) Shuttle diplomacy should not replace face-to-face conflict resolution unless cultural norms make cross-gender or face-to-face meetings inadvisable. Seeing the other party, noting their reactions, and hearing their voices as they state their concerns, can help people recognize the humanity in the other person, a perspective that is often distorted or missing in a conflict.

5. In what setting will the meetings occur?

The physical setting of a conflict resolution meeting can influence the process more than one would expect. There are several considerations when choosing the setting.

First, the setting should be a private space, free from interruptions by people, phones, or beepers.

Second, the space should not "belong" to either party. There is a psychological advantage to being on one's own turf, so it is best to be in a neutral space. If the conflict manager's office is private and free from interruptions, it gives the facilitator a helpful home court advantage. It is also wise to move people away from the location of their conflict, if possible. This provides the parties a fresh view.

Third, the space should be comfortable. It should have comfortable chairs, good lighting, and temperature control. Amenities like coffee, tea, and water make the face-to-face encounter feel a bit less hostile for the parties.

A fourth and critical consideration is seating arrangements. Use your authority as conflict manager to recommend an arrangement to the parties. Seating is important for two reasons.

First, when people are feeling uncomfortable or anxious about a face-to-face meeting, they often direct their remarks to the facilitator while the other party listens. This often helps people be frank and feel understood. Thus, the seating arrangement should make it easy to see and address the facilitator, especially early in the process.

The second reason for careful seating is related to eye contact in communication. Even when making direct eye contact is culturally acceptable for an individual, it is often uncomfortable when the individual feels strong negative emotions toward another person. Seating people at angles to one another allows them to choose when and whether to make eye contact. As emotions de-escalate, you are likely to see people who normally make eye contact initiate it again. In addition, parties will increasingly direct their comments to one another.

Round and square tables work best for this angled arrangement, but if you find you are at a long rectangular table, cluster people at one end and place parties diagonally across from one another. Be sure to position yourself near the parties. If you are at the opposite end of the table, the parties will have a hard time seeing and making eye contact with you. Also you will seem removed from the process, physically and psychologically. This will reduce your influence over events.

Put the parties at arm's length distance from one another, as this makes physical contact more difficult and eliminates a potential element of intimidation. If it is possible that intimidation could escalate into a physical conflict, arrange to meet in a space where people are nearby in case you have to call for help. See the tip on psychological and physical safety on pages 76-77 for more information.

Another option is open seating—a living room environment with armchairs or couches. Use this when you are sure people are comfortable with one another. Though more formal, tables offer people some psychological (and physical) protection. They form a barrier by setting a defined distance between people and also give people a place to set papers and rest their arms. Open seating sets a more informal tone and gives a feeling of openness, but does not offer the protection a table does. Your understanding of the people and the situation will guide you in arranging an appropriate setting.

6. How will you protect people's need for privacy and confidentiality?

Confidentiality is most important to the success of a conflict

Even if shuttle diplomacy is used for the entire time (and I don't believe this should happen in an organizational setting), people need to be brought together at least once to confirm the final resolution. This is necessary for two reasons. First, affirming the actual resolutions to the issues of the conflict allows everyone to be sure they share the same understanding. Second, people need to see each other face-to-face, as people, to reestablish rapport. Meeting face-to-face, sharing praise for resolving tough issues, and seeing the relief on each other's faces are steps toward reestablishing relationships.

One important caveat in shuttle diplomacy: Don't be an enabler. Many people would rather become dependent on an intermediary than face a person with whom they are in conflict. Use shuttle diplomacy sparingly. This is important for three reasons. First, shuttle diplomacy is time-consuming. Second, the conflict manager bears the onus of accurate communication between the parties and must distinguish between messages to the other party and confidential information. Finally, as much as possible, the parties should shoulder the responsibility of communicating their concerns and ideas. Doing so is part of reestablishing rapport.

Figure 5. Seating options for a conflict resolution meeting

Whether seating people around square, round, or rectangular tables, avoid placing the primary disputants directly across from each other.

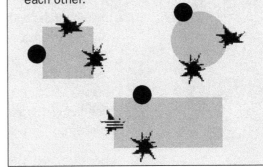

resolution process and must be stressed with all people involved. What is said in meetings, as well as the observations and opinions about what occurred in meetings, must be held confidential by everyone. (This means not even telling life partners or dearest friends.) The reason is simple. When people face someone with whom they have a conflict, they feel vulnerable about what may occur within the meeting. They also fear something they say or do will be represented to others in ways that will belittle or harm them. In order for parties to feel they can be both honest and direct in a conflict resolution setting, they must feel that what is said will remain private among the people involved in the process. As mentioned previously, confidentiality may not apply if issues of harassment, maltreatment, or certain illegalities are involved. If you are the organization's executive, it is your responsibility to take alternative actions, and it is not appropriate for the parties to discuss the matter.

In many mediations, mediators have people sign an agreement stating that what is said in the mediation will remain entirely confidential unless all parties jointly agree to release the information. If your situation warrants this formality, you will find a sample agreement to participate in conflict resolution in Appendix B (page 169). The agreement includes a statement on confidentiality. Most times, having people agree orally in each other's presence at the first meeting is enough. Remind all parties about this agreement at the end of the process.

The best laid plans...

You've heard from the parties, analyzed the conflict, and planned how you will convene a conflict resolution process. No doubt you're sure it's the best plan possible. It is important to have a plan, but remember that you can never entirely anticipate how conflict resolution processes will go. Therefore, be flexible. As you see the conflict resolution process unfold, you may want to modify your plans. Much like a navigator, you need to continually adjust the conflict resolution course to the changing events and climate of the conflict.

You and others involved may choose to take notes during meetings to help you remember what is said or make notes of things people want to ask or say. These notes should either be destroyed or kept by the facilitator (not the participants) after each meeting. When the conflict resolution process has ended, the notes should be destroyed. Similarly, flip charts or erasable boards used during meetings should be destroyed or erased.

When public information is part of the discussion and it is easily accessible through other sources, it does not become confidential simply because of the conflict resolution process. For example, if the organization's budget is discussed in a conflict resolution meeting and it is a readily available document, it is not confidential. However, what people had to say about the budget—their opinions and concerns about it—is private and confidential. So are observations of the participants' emotional states during that discussion. Personal matters, feelings, opinions, and the overall content of a conflict resolution meeting must be confidential. If there is any doubt about the public nature of information, it is wise to ask the participants if they have any concerns about the information being discussed outside of the conflict resolution process. If someone does have concerns, it is wisest to consider the information confidential.

Because this is an informal, cooperative process, no formal sanctions are built in for someone who breaks confidentiality. However, the process is embedded in an organization, which has sanction power. A party that breaks confidentiality risks the disapproval of the organization's leaders, loss of credibility, and subsequent loss of power. The breach could have long-term effects on opportunities for advancement and other organizational rewards and benefits. The knowledge of potential sanctions will deter most employees from breaching confidence.

If a serious breach occurs, end the conflict resolution process, because trust in both the process and the other parties will have seriously eroded. However, check with the parties before unilaterally ending the process. Shuttle diplomacy might be a fallback, if parties agree, although neither relationship nor identity conflicts are served by shuttle diplomacy. If this option is not feasible it is likely that more formal processes will be needed. At this point call your attorney for advice about how to proceed.

7. If this is a system-induced conflict, who needs to be consulted if changes in policy or procedure are part of the resolution?

If you determine that the conflict is related to a system in your organization, you may need to consult with an employee who oversees the system. You will probably have the employee's name listed on the conflict analysis worksheet under "other concerned people." You might involve them in one or more conflict resolution meetings if the parties agree. Or you might consult with them and bring the information to the discussions. If the person joins the conflict resolution meeting they too must agree to confidentiality.

All Hands on Deck!
Step 6: Educate Parties and Get Agreement to Participate

You've spotted the storm and figured out the best approach. Now it's "all hands on deck" as you gather the crew, explain what's coming—and be sure they're ready to help out!

There's no sense trying to resolve a conflict when the parties won't participate. In this step, you meet with the parties individually, tell them how the process will work, and ask them to agree to participate. Your motto regarding the conflict resolution process should be "no surprises."

As you meet with each person individually, tell them what to expect from the conflict resolution process—what the process steps are and what your role will be. Do it in detail and answer all their questions. Tell them both the positives and the negatives. Assure them that you will work to keep the discussions orderly and constructive. This private one-on-one meeting to explain the process and the ground rules is your opportunity to get people to agree to participate. It is also your chance to coach people, particularly the weaker party, about how to prepare for and fully participate in the conflict resolution meeting.

In the appendix you will find a checklist of all the process steps you will want to cover with the parties (see Process Steps Checklist, page 171). Use this checklist twice: first when you are educating the parties one-to-one and again at the opening of the first conflict management meeting between the parties. After you have made sure the person understands the process, you can ask him or her to agree to participate.

Sometimes people feel more able to participate in a conflict resolution process if they have the company of someone they trust. For this to happen, both parties must agree to the presence of others. Before and during the first meeting, you will need to clarify what role one or more additional people will play and then stick to whatever is decided. Usually the participation of trusted friends or advisers helps the process. However, such participation must be managed with care. If the parties agree to involve outsiders, follow these steps:

1. Clarify with the party and the party's adviser the exact role the adviser will play. For example, the adviser may offer support but be silent during the meeting; they may provide technical information in the meeting or at a caucus; or they may be full participants in the meeting. (Experience suggests not allowing full participation, even though it is an option. Advisers can escalate a conflict if, as they advocate for a friend, they disregard the impact of such advocacy on the future relationship of the parties.)

2. Be sure both parties agree on outside participation and on the type and amount of participation. Usually, the parties want equal treatment. Shuttle between the parties until you have complete agreement on the rules for adviser participation.

3. Be sure the advisers understand and agree to follow the rules before the first meeting.

4. At the first meeting, when all are present, repeat the rules that everyone has agreed the outsiders will follow. Be sure that everyone agrees once again to follow these rules; it is important that everyone witnesses the agreement in person. At this time parties and their advisers may choose to modify some rules. This is fine, as long as everyone at the meeting agrees to the modifications.

On rare occasions someone will object to an outside adviser during the meeting itself. If this happens, end the meeting and meet with the person privately to learn why they have had a change of heart. You will need to address their concerns or change your process.

Into the Gale!
Step 7: Conduct the Process

Ever the careful captain, you've made every preparation possible. Now you turn things over to the crew. Your job is to get things underway and direct the responses to the tempest around you.

Once the parties have agreed to participate, it's time to bring them together to tell their stories, listen to each other, generate possible solutions, and choose a resolution. Though there are many variations in the process, the basic steps are:

1. Set up the meeting environment
2. Open the meeting, set the ground rules for decorum, and explain the process steps
3. Have each party describe their experience uninterrupted
4. Invite questions for clarification of different experiences
5. Discuss and sort issues
6. Decide which issues to discuss first
7. Discuss issues and generate ideas for solutions within any known limitations
8. Review and modify the issues and possible solutions
9. Agree to a resolution
10. Formalize the agreement

1. Set up the meeting environment

Be sure to arrive before the participants so you can set up the meeting room. Whatever setting you choose, arrange it to improve the likelihood of resolution as discussed in Step 5: Design the Process. If by some accident you arrive after parties have seated themselves, start by rearranging people, if needed. As the facilitator you have that authority, so use it. Also be sure that participants are seated to shield them from bright windows, which cause eye strain. This discomfort can affect facial gestures and judgment.

Have pens, paper, a box of tissues, a flip chart or erasable board, and markers at the ready. Give the participants pens and paper so they can take notes to help them remember points they want to clarify or questions they want to ask. Remind them, though, that their notes are not for documentation and that you will either gather them at the end of each meeting or ask them to destroy them before leaving the room.

Place a box of tissues in easy reach of the participants. Remember, do not hand a tissue to a tearful participant, as you will seem sympathetic and partial to that party. Guard your impartiality by pointing to the tissues or by placing the box on the table near the person who seems to need them.

Sample rules for psychological and physical safety

You can set some simple rules to create a sense of psychological and physical safety that makes tense discussions more comfortable. Because many people don't accept rules unless they understand why they are important, reasons for the rules are placed in parentheses below.

Psychological Safety Rules
Decorum
- Encourage "I statements" (eliminates accusatory statements and assumptions)

- No accusatory statements (makes people defensive, escalates emotions)

- No pushing hot buttons or making personal digs (is shaming, escalates emotions, sidetracks issues)

- No language that either party finds offensive, such as swearing or name calling (escalates emotions, obscures issues)

- No offensive gestures (escalates emotions, obscures issues)

- No interrupting (breaks continuity of process, makes people defensive)

Control
- Permission to take or call for breaks in the discussions (allows people to release stress, emote privately)

- Seating so that parties have a choice about making eye contact (creates privacy of emotions and reactions, empowers parties to choose when to visually relate to one another)

(continued)

2. Open the meeting

When opening the meeting, your first job will be to reassure parties, decrease their anxiety, and assure that everyone knows they are working from the same rules. The first step in opening a meeting is to welcome everyone, make necessary introductions, and explain the process steps for the meeting. You will have done this once before in individual meetings with the parties (Step 6). Doing it again has several benefits:

- Everyone hears the same information at the same time.

- Introductory comments give people time to calm down. Take your time explaining the process steps (See Step 6) and answering questions. This may take up to a half hour.

- You can reassure the participants about your own faith in the process and their abilities to resolve the situation. Say only things you actually believe, but do try to be positive while acknowledging the challenge everyone at the table faces.

- You can build the parties' trust in you by explaining what you have already done as part of the process—information gathering, individual meetings with parties, thinking through the process, and so forth. Be sure to describe these activities in a way that establishes you as fair and even-handed and does not give any specifics you have learned.

- If appropriate, you can talk about alternatives to settling the dispute. With luck, participants will view the process on which you are about to embark as the most promising.

Next, discuss the basic rules that all conflict resolution meetings follow:

- People must speak respectfully to one another. For information about this, see the tip on Sample Rules for Physical and Psychological Safety to the left.

- A common way to ensure respectful dialogue is to have people phrase their thoughts from their own perspective as "I statements," because such phrasing makes accusations difficult. (For information on constructing "I statements," see Limiting Belittling and Blaming, pages 103-104.)

- Participants are expected to speak and act in good faith—to tell the truth as they know it and to agree only to actions they are willing to do.

- All people in the meeting must keep all the information confidential. If parties want to sign a confidentiality agreement, this is the time to do it.

Find out if the parties want to modify the ground rules. Ask them to discuss and agree on how they will interact in this process. This can give them their first experience in finding common ground, in making an agreement, and in developing hope about their larger dispute.

Next, discuss the meeting mechanics:

- Clarify the role of people attending the meeting (friends and advisers who are not parties).
- Let everyone know the time the meeting will end.
- Explain that people may ask to take breaks or request caucuses with the facilitator at any time. Remind them what caucuses are and how they work. (Instructions for conducting caucuses are at the end of this step on page 78.)

Finally, explain the order of the process you have designed. You will find a checklist of substeps in the appendix on page 171. Descriptions of these substeps follow.

- Meeting space is in neutral setting (no home turf advantage)

Privacy
- No interruptions from outside people, telephones, pagers (continuity of process, privacy)
- No discussion of what is said with others—not even spouses or close friends (reduces escalation of emotions, distrust, misinformation)
- No meeting notes leave the meeting room (avoids escalation of emotions, distrust, misinformation)

Physical Safety Rules
- No weapons
- Seat people arm's length apart (makes shoving or hitting less likely)
- Give parties easy entry and exit from the meeting space (provides a sense of control regarding involvement in the meeting; reduces close contact among parties)
- Meet in a private space where others are nearby (help is in easy reach)

3. Have each party describe their experience uninterrupted

This is the opportunity for the parties to hear each other's concerns in full in a structured, safe environment. Have one party state their understanding of the issues, what is personally important about the issues, and if they choose, their feelings about the conflict. Rarely do people need much coaching in this step. They have practiced by telling the conflict manager many of these things in their private meeting. Once one party has described their experience, the other party does the same—also uninterrupted.

Parties usually want to interrupt each other to debate points. I recommend that they write down their questions and comments about each other's perspectives while listening, and save them for the next step. This eliminates interruptions and helps each party remember their comments for the next step, in which discussion is encouraged.

4. Invite questions for clarification of different experiences

After each party has given their view, both the facilitator and the parties can ask for clarification. This step can be contentious because the parties want to tell each other why they are wrong. The point is to understand each other's perspective, not debate it. However, some debate usually occurs; if it is limited, it is not a problem. Be prepared to enforce the ground rules for decorum, however.

How to conduct breaks and caucuses

Simple breaks can be called by any participant for comfort purposes, time to think, or when people become weary, distracted, or overcome by emotion.

Caucuses—private, confidential meetings between any people involved in the conflict resolution process can be used when:

- The discussion seems repetitive
- You sense "missing" information
- You cannot quite follow the logic or sequence of statements, even after asking for and getting clarification
- You sense emotions escalating
- You think people might need to vent

In a caucus you can get clarification, test out your ideas and observations, or have the party test out thoughts they are hesitant to express at the table. You can role play the situation, or coach them about how to express themselves. If they cannot bring themselves to speak, you can—with the party's permission—carry the idea to the other party. If the party does not care to present the information, you may not do so. This will break confidentiality, and you will lose their trust.

When a party uses a caucus to vent during a tense situation, avoid agreeing or disagreeing with the party even as you affirm their feelings. Occasionally you can present another perspective as a way to reframe the situation, but do so carefully and sparingly or your reframing will be perceived as partiality.

Anyone participating in a conflict resolution meeting can call a caucus. During a caucus, the conflict manager meets independently and confidentially with each party for the same amount of time. If this does not occur, the party you did not meet with may doubt your impartiality. Keep caucuses relatively brief, or the waiting party may become anxious.

5. Discuss and sort issues

In this step the parties, with your help, try to untangle the web of misunderstanding and disagreement and break it into distinct (but often interrelated) issues. Write the issues on the flip chart or erasable board. Parties may modify or change what you write, which helps them clarify their thoughts. As facilitator you are likely to use your skills in seeking interests, reframing issues, and uncovering the interests embedded in positions. (You'll learn about these skills in Chapter Three.) Once all the positions and interests have been identified and listed, you are prepared to prioritize them. Often this is a good time to suggest a break, noting the progress already made.

6. Decide which issues to discuss first

Depending on the situation, there may be a logical sequence in which to address related issues. Go with what the parties choose. However, it is generally wise to start with an issue that's easy to resolve—either because it is simple or because people have little disagreement about it. Getting even a simple issue tentatively settled creates a feeling of optimism and makes tackling harder issues more promising. Use the flip chart or erasable board for this step.

7. Discuss issues and generate ideas for solutions within any known limitations

Now we move into the integrative part of the conflict resolution process. Parties begin to discuss single issues in the order they determined and begin to generate possible solutions, each time evaluating whether the solutions address their interests. This step is repeated for each issue. If the parties get stuck on an issue, put that one on hold and move on to the next one. As momentum builds toward resolution, there is often a better chance of successfully resolving the sticky point later. There is no need to finalize the solution for each issue at this point; the group will review all the solutions and how they fit together in the next step.

This is the creative part of the process. To help parties explore potential solutions, you can reframe issues, ask "dumb" questions, and politely challenge their assumptions. Other techniques for expanding creativity are described in Chapter Three.

8. Review and modify the issues and possible solutions

Once the parties have discussed possible solutions for all the issues, they can review them as a whole and modify them as necessary. This is also the time to discuss concerns about implementation or follow-up. Sometimes at this juncture new issues suddenly arise. This happens because an interest was not addressed in a previously devised solution. This is rarely the result of someone being obstreperous or creating a spiral conflict. When people are intensely emotional, the conflict seems like a jumble of issues, and they are not clear about what interests are really important to them. As the integration phase proceeds people grow more optimistic, more creative, and more clear about what is important to them—and an undiscovered interest suddenly surfaces. Be patient and work on the newly surfaced interest as you did on earlier issues.

9. Agree to a resolution

When all the pieces have come together, the parties agree to a resolution. To be sure everyone has the same understanding of the agreement, the facilitator can draft the resolution and have the parties refine it. Reading an agreed-upon resolution seems to encourage people to be sure they understand the meaning of its language. This can help prevent future misinterpretations.

10. Formalize the agreement

There are several options for formalizing the agreement. The facilitator can read it and get oral agreement, the parties can finalize it with a handshake, or they can sign a written letter of understanding. Even though the agreement is not really a formal document, there are times when people feel more confident when they have an agreement in writing. (A Letter of Understanding is included in Appendix B, page 170.)

Shore Leave!
Step 8: Celebrate and Check In

You've weathered the storm. There were creaks and groans, but the ship made it through in good shape, ready to sail into port. Ever the thoughtful captain, you know it's time for your crew to celebrate their hard work and success. They deserve it—and a celebration will prepare them to succeed in coming storms, too.

When people work through a conflict, there is reason

to celebrate. Given that everyone wants to get back to business, this is an easy step to forget. Don't. View it as an investment in people's willingness and abilities to resolve future conflicts, preferably on their own.

A celebration ends what was likely a difficult set of interactions on a positive note. Base the celebration on the situation and people. It need be no more elaborate than starting a round of thank-yous or handshakes. It usually includes the facilitator praising the parties' efforts.

Check in

Finally, set a future time—a week, a month, or a few months—when you will check in with the parties about how their agreement is holding up. Sometimes parties make this part of their agreement, but even if they don't, it is wise to check in. You are most likely to find everyone viewing their conflict as ancient history and your query will be dismissed with a quick response of "just fine." It does happen, however, that some aspect of an agreement is not working. This gives you and the parties an opportunity to fine-tune the agreement to stave off future problems.

CHAPTER THREE

Sailing Hazardous Waters
Conflict Management Skills and Exercises

IN A STORM, heavy seas threaten the ship. Winds and waves shift unpredictably while rocks and reefs surprise the unprepared. The skillful captain must learn to navigate amidst these hazards.

People's emotions, previous experiences, and assumptions flood their perceptions during the storms of conflict. A conflict manager's job is to help people ride the waves, avoid submerged dangers, and find the best course. Much of what a conflict manager does is help people truly hear and understand one another.

This chapter presents explanations of and exercises for skills and techniques key to successful conflict management. Much of this will be familiar, because it concerns communications—an area most effective leaders already understand. You may possess many of them, but may not have named them or considered how they can be best used to help resolve conflict.

The skills you will learn in this chapter include:

- Affirming and Restating
- Mirroring Body Language
- Asking Neutral Questions
- Assisting Upset People
- Identifying Interests
- Reframing Issues
- Limiting Belittling and Blaming
- Breaking Stalemates

I believe these are the most effective and versatile of many conflict resolution skills. To develop or improve these skills you have to practice them. Try them on your kids, your friends, or the family dog—but practice them out loud! As you hear yourself communicating like this, you will gain confidence. The more naturally you can use these techniques in a conflict resolution setting (with its tense and awkward moments), the more effective and helpful you will be. So please—practice!

Affirming and Restating

In conflicts, frustrations mount when people think they aren't being understood or taken seriously. Affirming and restating are techniques that help people know that they are heard and understood. An affirming statement is one that indicates that the listener understands the speaker's emotions. The listener uses restating to recast or repeat the speaker's ideas to indicate that he or she recognizes, takes seriously, and understands (not necessarily agrees with) what the speaker has said.

Affirming validates feelings that the speaker names or implies. You, as the listener, make affirming remarks that articulate an emotion you hear implied in the speaker's choice of words, tone of voice, or gestures. Many people have a limited vocabulary for describing their emotions, so naming a feeling acknowledges its validity and allows the speaker to decide if, indeed, that is how they feel. Affirming remarks are often cast as questions, rather than statements, so as not to presuppose knowing the speaker's feelings. For example, if the speaker's voice quality and body language seem to indicate frustration, asking if the speaker feels frustrated gives them a chance to confirm or correct that impression.

Restating lets you check your understanding of the speaker. When people feel that their ideas are being discounted or misinterpreted, their frustration and anger grow. Restating has the opposite effect. Repeating the speaker's key ideas in different words helps the speaker know that the ideas are clearly understood or, if they are misunderstood, gives the speaker the opportunity to further clarify. This reassures the speaker that they are being heard and taken seriously and relieves anger and frustration. Much of the emotion people bring to the conflict resolution table results from their feeling that they and their ideas are not valued or understood.

When to use affirming and restating

Affirming and restating help in several different phases of the conflict management process. When used to gather information, these techniques can establish your rapport with the parties and deepen your understanding of the issues, emotions, and scope of the conflict.

Restating is particularly helpful during conversations between the parties. People in conflict tend to attribute negative characteristics to each other and withdraw empathy. They hear each other through a negative filter. Words that would seem innocuous or even helpful from a neutral person seem negative or unacceptable when they come from the opposing party. When the conflict manager states the opposing party's message, the listener often better understands and accepts it because they are not filtering the conflict manager's language negatively. Restating is often used both to clarify what was said and to help the listener hear the ideas in a different voice and in different words.

Affirming and restating put the parties in conflict more at ease. They decrease the fears and frustrations people have about being discounted or misunderstood, and they create empathy (not sympathy) between listener and speaker.

The exercises on pages 84-86 will help you practice these skills.

Mirroring Body Language

Mirroring is a form of body language that people use, often unconsciously, to convey their rapport with others. The next time you see people deeply engaged in conversation, note their body positions and movement. You will see that they tend to sit or stand in similar positions as they speak and that when one person moves, the other will move in a similar way. If one crosses their arms, the other will do something similar; if one leans forward, so will the other. Or note that at relaxed meetings or meals, when one person takes a sip of coffee, the others quickly do the same. All of this looks rather like a dance, and in some ways it is. Like dance partners, partners in conversation make complementary movements to send one another cues that they are engaged and harmonious.

So what does mirroring have to do with people in conflict? Because mirroring is largely an unconscious act, signs of mirroring can help you see when the barriers of fear and defensiveness are beginning to break down and parties are starting to establish rapport. You can also consciously mirror the parties' positive body language during conflict resolution sessions to help defuse fear. When you do this, each party feels that there is someone present with whom they have rapport. Mirroring also lets you convey empathy with the parties without agreeing or disagreeing with their ideas or concerns.

During information gathering, use mirroring to set up rapport and trust and to build confidence that the process will be handled fairly. The exercise on page 86 will improve your understanding of this technique.

No sympathy!

Affirming statements must be carefully worded because they should not express sympathy. Sympathetic statements imply an alliance between the speaker and listener. But the conflict manager should be allied with no one—neutrality is essential to maintaining the trust of all parties. The following examples of affirming statements show empathy, not sympathy:

- Let me see, when _____ occurs you feel _____?
- I see that this is a very important issue for you.
- So, that is why the matter is upsetting?
- It makes you feel _____ when _____?
- You sound very serious about that.
- It seems you have given this a lot of thought.
- It sounds like this has been very difficult for you.

Avoid using sympathetic statements like these:

- I am sorry that _____.
- Something like that happened to me: _____.
- That's awful.
- Too bad.
- I really understand.
- That's bad.

Also, do not parrot a person's words when affirming or restating. Parroting makes most people feel manipulated. Also avoid phrases like "I hear you saying _____," which have been made ineffective by overuse. Use words and phrases natural to you; these show you understand someone's meaning or feelings without sounding phony.

Asking Neutral Questions and Making Neutral Statements

You need to be skillful at asking neutral questions to avoid inadvertently conveying judgments while gathering or clarifying information about a conflict. The parties will be listening to you keenly for implications of judgment, in part because they are accustomed to bringing their conflicts before an authority figure for resolution.

EXERCISE

Affirming Statements

The following exercises will help you use affirming statements during conflict management. First identify the emotion or emotions the speaker might be displaying, and then make two different affirming statements that convey that you recognize their state of emotion. Be sure to choose words and phrases natural to your own way of speaking.

Example

As an employee tells you about a longtime "personality conflict" at work, you see tears welling up in their eyes.

Name the emotion(s): sadness, frustration, or anger

Statement 1: This is really affecting you, isn't it?

Statement 2: Does it make you sad (angry, frustrated)?

Exercises

1. The tone of voice of someone speaking with you sounds increasingly constricted and their words become increasingly terse.

   Name the emotion(s):

   Statement 1:

   Statement 2:

2. A person is hesitating and fidgeting as they begin a discussion with you.

   Name the emotion(s):

   Statement 1:

   Statement 2:

3. A person in a heated moment pushes their chair away from the table and leans back.

   Name the emotion(s):

   Statement 1:

   Statement 2:

4. During a conversation, you note that one person is sighing heavily.

   Name the emotion(s):

   Statement 1:

   Statement 2:

5. You see a staff member rubbing their temples and forehead during a meeting.

   Name the emotion(s):

   Statement 1:

   Statement 2:

Restating Meaning

In each of the situations below, make one statement to help the listener know that you understand his or her meaning. Make a second statement to solicit more information.

Example 1

In telling you about a conversation with a board member, a program director says, "And then she told me to write a speech she can give when she attends neighborhood meetings. She thinks I have nothing to do but be her personal speechwriter. That's not my job."

Statement 1: Do you think she's looking for help organizing information about our programs so that she'll feel confident presenting it to neighborhood groups? Do you get the sense that public speaking is hard for her?

Statement 2: She wants you to give information about your program to present to neighborhood organizations? Do you think she is worried about not really understanding the program well enough to explain it and answer questions?

Example 2

Heaving a big sigh, a manager begins to tell you about a complicated series of events that led up to an angry exchange between him and a volunteer. "When I told him that he cannot let the person he is mentoring sleep overnight at his home, he said that all the rules he has to follow in this organization are stupid and that he thinks this organization is a big bureaucracy that doesn't really help people. Then he stalked out."

Statement 1: So he is angry that our rules limit his choice of activities with the person he is mentoring? Do you think he understands the reasons for some of our rules?

Statement 2: He wants the person he is mentoring to sleep in his home. Do you think he would be open to exploring some other way to have time together?

Exercises

1. An angry board member complains to you about the way the chair of the board's planning committee runs the committee meetings. "I think that she and the members of the committee have gotten together in advance to get what they want. She pushes through her own agenda with their support and never really lets anyone else speak. I'm wasting my time on this committee."

Statement 1:

Statement 2:

(continued)

2. A disappointed grant applicant tells you his concerns about the process your agency uses to make funding decisions. "I think it's not a fair process. The grant panel just gives money to their friends."

Statement 1:

Statement 2:

3. A service recipient confronts you in the hall with a series of complaints about a staff member's behavior. "Every time I meet with her she answers the phone and makes me wait through these long phone calls. And then when she does talk to me she is always in a rush, so I feel like I can't ask all my questions and like she is trying to get rid of me."

Statement 1:

Statement 2:

4. An annoyed employee of an agency that regulates your nonprofit calls to say that funding is being withheld until missing reports are filed with the agency.

Statement 1:

Statement 2:

EXERCISE

Mirroring

Here are two ways to become aware and comfortable with mirroring. The first is to simply be a keen observer. The next time you are waiting in a public place, take time to observe the people around you. Watch for mirroring between people engaged in conversations. Can you surmise the tenor of their conversations by their movements? (If you have ever had fantasies about being a spy, this is your chance to live them out!)

Second, experiment while talking with friends and relatives. Note how you and they use mirroring as part of the conversation. Consciously try to mirror them and see how it is received. Or if you want to push the experiment a little further, consciously avoid mirroring and see how and when your partner reacts. (Warning! This latter can be risky, so pick your guinea pig with care and remember to tell them what you were doing later.)

Despite your explanation of neutrality, people often view any conflict manager as an authority figure and either hope he or she will "be on their side" or fear he or she will "be on the other's side." (Note that as a nonprofit leader you are on a "side"—the side of your organization's welfare.)

The natural tendency for parties to attempt to win you over often has a positive side effect: Because each party wants you to perceive them as the "good guy," each will try to be reasonable and avoid outbursts. However, no matter how parties behave, you must be impartial and evenhanded at the most minute level. You will need to be careful to spend similar amounts of time talking with each party, making eye contact with each (if that's important to the culture you're in), and generally demonstrating your impartiality through your actions, word choice, and intonation. Even handing someone a tissue can sometimes be perceived by the other party as being partial!

In dispute resolution terminology this quality is called remaining neutral. Being neutral does not mean that you have no feelings or ideas about the different issues or people with whom you are dealing. It means not conveying your feelings and ideas to the parties. Establishing your neutrality and trustworthiness from the start of the process is essential—guarding it throughout is critical.

You can learn to ask questions and make statements in a way that conveys your impartiality. The well-known journalist's questions, who, what, where, when, why, and how, are generally quite neutral. However, if inadvertently colored by vocal intonations, these words can also impart judgmental messages such as doubt, outrage, sympathy, or incredulity—all the types of messages a conflict manager wants to guard against.

Neutral affirmations

Statements like the following can be validating and affirming without making a judgment about the issues or the people involved.

- "I can see this is a very serious matter to you."

- "I understand that this is very important to you."

- "I see that this is very upsetting."

- "You have thought this matter through."

- "Your ideas are very helpful to my understanding the issues."

Also, be careful not to phrase your questions like a television prosecutor. (As in, "So, just why were you complaining to the board chair, Mr. X?") Even if your questions are not judgmental in themselves, questions phrased this way raise people's anxiety and put them on the defensive. (Save these questions for the mystery you always planned to write.) Similarly, asking detailed questions about events people cannot easily recall accurately (like exact dates or dollar amounts) puts people on the defensive. If you need this kind of information, give people time to refer to the resources they need to get you accurate information.

Legalistic language can imply blame or judgment, too. Whenever possible avoid words like whereabouts, the accused, culprit, witness, defendant, victim, alleged, and case. These words are not neutral, at least in the informal kind of conversations we are talking about, because they raise the specter of the courtroom where judgments are made and blame is assigned.

Following are examples of neutral and judgmental questions and statements. An exercise follows.

Neutral: What happened then?
Judgmental: I can't believe it! Then what happened?

Neutral: How did you feel when _____?
Judgmental: I bet you really felt awful when _____

Neutral: Were there others who saw or heard that too?
Judgmental: Were there witnesses?

Neutral: How did you come to that conclusion?
Judgmental: How do you know that?

EXERCISE

Asking Neutral Questions and Making Neutral Statements

To better understand the impact of intonation, practice what not to do during conflict management. Either alone or with a friend, try to use your voice intonations to give as many meanings as you can to each of these words: who, what, where, when, why, how. Try a number of intonations and have your partner tell you what he or she thinks you con-veyed. Consciously using your voice to change the meaning of these words will sensitize you to how easily you can convey unintended messages. Next, see how many different meanings you can convey using the following questions and statements.

- Why did you do that?
- How do you know?
- Who did that?
- Really.
- No.

Assisting Upset People

In Chapter One I described how under stress a person's whole body goes on alert and the limbic portion of the brain prepares to respond to danger, while the activity in the cortex, the "thinking" part of the brain, slows. When you encounter an upset person, you are dealing with this phenomenon.

Complicating this physical response is a cultural one. Our organizational norms are strongly influenced by Northern European cultures where calm and dispassionate communication is highly valued. We have incorporated this preference into much of our public behavior—including the norms of the workplace. With this preference has come the belief that people who are expressing strong emotions are irrational, less intelligent, or unprofessional—even possibly out-of-control. Seeing someone express strong emotions, particularly in a work setting where such expression is unconventional, usually makes people uncomfortable or even downright scared. This reaction tends to make the emoting person feel a sense of urgency themselves; it can even trigger a flight or fight reaction. At the least, people often feel a need to calm the "emotional" person immediately.

Displays of strong emotion may not faze you. Be aware, however, that not everyone in your organization will be comfortable with them. It's important that you teach staff not to be frightened by other people's emotions, not to discount an upset person's intelligence and professionalism, and most important, how to listen to and assist an upset person.

When it's time for tea

A university dean was a tea lover and kept an electric teapot, many exotic teas, and a china tea set in her office. Whenever an upset staff member came to her office, she offered them tea. During the time it took to boil the water, select and brew the tea, and pour it into the delicate cups, the upset person often began to calm down. According to the dean, this small calming ritual also helped place the problem in a different perspective, where it could be discussed with more objectivity. Intuitively and to great effect, she had employed the technique I am suggesting.

If you value calm, dispassionate communication, you will be battling your own discomfort and desire to have things calm down quickly. It is important to recognize that in many other cultures the norms allow people to be much more expressive in public settings and that this display of emotion is unrelated to the person's intelligence or ability to make sense. As a matter of fact, allowing a person to emote—without giving them the sense that you are trying to stifle them—is an effective way to enable people to calm down. So if people are not harming themselves or others, learn to allow them to express strong emotions and withhold your judgment about their capabilities, professionalism, or rationality. You can help them by giving them your attention and providing a safe environment for them to emote.

The techniques for helping people calm themselves are familiar. This list is a reminder of different methods available. Select techniques from the list using your best judgment about the situation at hand.

Create an environment to establish calm

- Bring the upset person to a quiet place, especially if the interaction is occurring in a public, crowded, or noisy space. Consider your own safety, too, as you select a quiet place.

- Speak softly (even if people are yelling); they will in time quiet down.

- Invite an upset person to sit down, and sit down yourself.

- Offer something to eat or drink (nonalcoholic).

- Assure the person that you want to understand and help.

- Give your name and ask the person her or his name (if you don't know each other).

Help the upset person tell his or her story and feel listened to

- Let them tell you why they are upset—hear them out fully.

- Don't judge or interrupt.

- Indicate understanding (not necessarily agreement) by nodding and by making affirming sounds or statements.

- Ask questions for clarification.

Use active listening techniques

- Make encouraging comments like "I really want to hear what you have to say" or "Tell me about that."

- Ask neutral clarifying questions such as "Can you tell me more about _____?" and the usual "Who? what? when? where? why? and how?"

- Restate what you understand using questions such as "So you are saying _____happened?" or "Do you mean _____?"

- Validate their emotions and the importance of the situation to them with a statement such as "I can see this is very difficult for you."

- Summarize your understanding of the situation: "Am I right that you are saying _____?"

Use body language as well as words

- Lean toward the person slightly.

- Have an open stance or sitting position—avoid crossed arms and legs.

- Avoid fiddling or fidgeting.

- Look the person in the eye, if it is culturally appropriate.

- Mirror the person's body language. (See "Mirroring Body Language" on page 83 for more information.)

Convey neutral empathy and understanding

Probably most important to an upset person is that they feel that their listener is an advocate or neutral, but definitely not an adversary. It is possible to remain neutral about a situation and still convey empathy and understanding. Feeling unheard or patronized will make people more upset—so truly listen and be genuine in what you say.

- Use words and phrases that you genuinely feel, like "I want to help you straighten out the situation," "I can see that this is very frustrating," or "I understand your concerns."

- Offer some sort of immediate assistance if possible, even if it is something very small.

• Give the person a set time at which they can expect you to contact them with further help—or ask them to call you directly if they have not heard from you by a specified date.

This exercise will help you assist upset people.

EXERCISE

Assisting Upset People

In this exercise, three people work together in a number of role plays, the scripts for which follow. One takes the role of an "upset person," the second is a "staff person" who listens to the problem, and the third is an "observer." Each participant should be given only the information in the script for the role assigned to him or her—that is, the staff person should not have any of the background that the upset person receives. As in real life, no one in the interaction has all the information—they have to get information from each other.

When the scene is finished, the observer should state which techniques worked effectively and suggest others that might have been tried. Also, it is often enlightening to ask the "upset person" how different approaches made him or her feel. Even though everyone knows this is playacting, the person playing the upset role still gets a sense of whether certain statements or actions made them feel calmer or more upset. Finally, the people in the exercise should change parts so that each person gets a chance to play the upset person, listener, and observer. Use a different script when changing parts. This keeps the information fresh and ensures that the actors will know only their part of the scenario.

By practicing a variety of techniques, you will have more skills to draw on in a real life situation

and you'll gain experience using techniques that are less natural to you. Remember, don't rush to solve the person's problem; learn to let them emote and to listen. Create a calming environment, and then help them with their problem.

Following are four scenarios based on real situations. You might also want to write some of your own based on experiences in your nonprofit.

Scenario 1: The "bad neighbor" nonprofit

Upset person

You have been a home owner in the Grove neighborhood for over forty years. A nonprofit funded by the United Way bought a house on the block last year and ever since, seedy-looking men have been wandering the neighborhood. Several of the longtime neighbors and you have discussed the trouble the nonprofit's shelter is causing. There have been five instances of these unkempt people littering, sleeping, and even defecating in neighbors' yards. One of your neighbors says he has complained to the nonprofit, but nothing has changed.

You are sitting in your sunroom when suddenly a seedy man peers into your window. He proceeds to trample your flower bed as he walks through your yard. Frightened, you watch from your win-

(continued)

dow as he enters the shelter. This is the last straw for you, and you decide you must confront someone. You have seen the United Way symbol on the door of the house and decide to go directly to the United Way offices. As a United Way donor, you want them to stop funding this trouble-making nonprofit shelter. You ask for an allocations staff member, and as you describe your experience you begin to cry uncontrollably.

Staff person

A person enters the United Way office asking to speak to a staff member in charge of allocations. You are called to come and meet with the person. As the person begins to talk they burst into uncontrollable tears.

Observer

Watch the interaction and note the techniques the staff person uses to assist the upset person. How does the upset person respond to the different techniques the staff person tries? After the scene is completed, tell the participants what seemed to work and what didn't. Ask them how they felt while doing the exercise.

Scenario 2: The group home incident

Upset person

You are a volunteer in a group home and have worked hard for the organization over the last five years. While most of your experiences have been positive, you just had a frightening one. On your last visit, one of the residents grabbed you around the neck. You instinctively pulled away and in doing so, you pushed the resident. As she fell she hit her head on a table and went into convulsions on the floor. At the time you pulled away an attendant saw you push the resident. Afraid the attendant would accuse you of abuse, you left the group home confused and

drove home, your knees shaking all the way. An accusation of abuse could have a terrible effect on your future, since you're running for the school board—a race that has turned very controversial. You know if this incident becomes public, it will be used against you. You turn the car around, return to the group home, and go directly to the executive director's office.

Staff person

One of your most reliable volunteers rushes into your office. By the look on their face you can see something is terribly wrong, but the person seems somewhat in control.

Observer

Watch the interaction and note the techniques the staff person uses to assist the upset person. How does the upset person respond to the different techniques the staff person tries? After the scene is completed, tell the participants what seemed to work and what didn't. Ask them how they felt while doing the exercise.

Scenario 3: The lewd comments incident

Upset person

You enter your manager's office and ask to speak privately. Your manager agrees. You feel terribly embarrassed, but you don't know where else to turn for help. Over the last two weeks you have been receiving telephone calls in the middle of the night. The caller has made suggestive and lewd remarks to you. Though frightened, you have not discussed the calls with anyone at work. Today in your desk, you found a rose and a note repeating some of the remarks the caller has made to you. You are sure that someone in the workplace is the caller and you are very frightened. You feel extremely confused and don't know what to do.

(continued)

Staff person

One of your employees comes into your office, asks to speak with you, and shuts the door. The employee looks strained and hesitant.

Observer

Watch the interaction and note the techniques the staff person uses to assist the upset person. How does the upset person respond to the different techniques the staff person tries? After the scene is completed, tell the participants what seemed to work and what didn't. Ask them how they felt while doing the exercise.

Scenario 4: Ganging up

Upset person

Your son, Sam, recently entered North End Kids Club for his after-school care. Several days in the past two weeks, Sam has come home from the Kids Club really upset. He says that the other boys are calling him names like "fag" and "sissy" because he doesn't join the rough and tumble games they play at recess. You know that Sam is a gentle boy who prefers art and board games to sports. When he came home yesterday, you saw large bruises on his arms. When asked about the bruises, he told that some boys in his group ganged up on him at recess and "popped" him several times. They told him they didn't want gays in their group. You are very upset and can't believe the teachers permit this behavior to go on at the club. You've never met Sam's teacher, but have heard she has an excellent reputation. Still upset, you stop to talk to Sam's teacher when you pick Sam up at the end of the day.

Staff person

You have been a teacher at North End Kids Club for eight years and are a well-liked and respected member of the staff. A new boy, Sam, joined your group this past month. He seems a little shy, but is bright and interested in many of the group's activities. You've noticed some increased teasing and joking among the boys in the last few weeks, and Sam seems to be having some trouble integrating into the group. He has not said anything to you about it. Your past experience tells you that things will settle down soon, and he will be accepted in the group. At the end of the day as the children are leaving, a person who you think is Sam's parent asks to speak with you. The person is clearly upset.

Observer

Watch the interaction and note the techniques the staff person uses to assist the upset person. How does the upset person respond to the different techniques the staff person tries? After the scene is completed, tell the participants what seemed to work and what didn't. Ask them how they felt while doing the exercise.

Identifying Interests

Identifying interests is one of the most important skills a conflict manager can use. It requires listening keenly, reading body language accurately, and sensing implied or unstated meanings in people's communications. Identifying interests can be challenging because of our American tendency to rush to solutions and action, and because in typical communication much information is left unsaid, leaving room for misinterpretation.

The rush to solutions

American culture is action oriented, and we tend to move quickly to solutions when handling a problem. In fact, as Americans we frequently describe a problem as the lack of the solution we have identified. In reality, our identified solution is likely to be one of many possibilities for addressing the problem. Because of our cultural propensity to move to solutions quickly, the real problem, needs, or concerns—the interests—often remain unstated.

"To receive a cup of tea we must hold an empty cup."

Zen master

The parties in conflict each develop their own solutions to the conflict, based on their unique frames of reference—their perceptions and the information available to them. Because people's perceptions and information often differ, it is likely that their solutions will differ as well. And because people habitually talk about a problem as the lack of the solution they have identified, they disagree over which solution should be implemented. Thus they often view each other as irrationally blocking the solution. This deepens the conflict.

To help people find the most acceptable solution to a conflict, you need to help them think about what issues or concerns (interests) are addressed by their proposed solutions (positions). This process can lead to a new and often better solution and to a durable resolution to the conflict.

With some experience, you can learn to recognize the interests underneath the typical problem statement or position. The following examples illustrate the difference.

Problem statement: We need more money if we are to start this badly needed new program.

Real interest: We want to meet an important need we see in the community.

Problem statement: I need a bigger office. The other staff all have better offices.

Real interest: I want to feel that the organization values me as much as other employees.

Problem statement: This memo to the board of directors has to be perfect.

Real interest: I want my board's trust and respect, and I want them to accept my ideas.

The exercise on pages 96-97 will help you learn to identify interests.

Shorthand communications

Most of us talk (and to some extent write) in an abbreviated way—in communication shorthand. The more familiar we are with a language and culture, and the better we know an individual, the easier it is to understand the intrinsic meanings of their shorthand communications and the more efficient and rapid is our communication.

But shorthand communication often leaves important ideas unstated. The listener is challenged to guess, correctly or incorrectly, about what those ideas might be. When people find themselves in conflict—emotionally distanced from others and feeling threatened or defensive—correctly guessing the unstated ideas in shorthand communications becomes much more difficult. Further, people have the tendency to guess wrong because they attribute negative motives or characteristics to the people with whom they are in conflict. Finally, the parties' real interests are frequently left unstated in shorthand communications.

You can help parties fill in the blanks in their shorthand communications and bring out unstated interests. Once these are on the table, parties can develop solutions based on more complete and accurate perceptions and information.

Have you ever been in a staff meeting when someone said, "We tried that before and it didn't work."? This is an example of shorthand communication in which the speaker omits the circumstances surrounding the proposed solution when it was previously attempted. Old-timers may be aware of these circumstances, but new staff members are not. The shorthand communication stops progress. Next time someone says "we tried that before," ask the person to explain why the idea didn't work in the past. This fills in the information missing from the shorthand communication. The group can then decide whether the solution might be useful in the current situation.

EXERCISE

Identifying Interests

Consider the following statements and identify the implied concerns or needs. Remember, the concerns can be substantive, procedural, relationship-based, or identity-based.

Example

"That funder requires us to collect all this useless data."

Possible interests:

- I don't understand the value of the data we are required to collect.
- Collecting this data takes a lot of my time.
- I don't like collecting this data.
- I feel forced to use my time on an activity I don't value.

Exercise

1. "The finance department does not keep information in a useful format."

   Possible interests:

2. "Executive directors can be really out of touch."

   Possible interests:

3. "It's not fair that managers get to take long lunch hours, but we secretaries get only thirty minutes."

   Possible interests:

(continued)

4. "I need a day off."

   Possible interests:

5. "The leadership never involves us in decisions."

   Possible interests:

6. "These meetings are a waste of my time."

   Possible interests:

7. "I want a promotion."

   Possible interests:

Reframing Issues

Each person filters and understands events through their unique conceptual lenses—personal history, culture, race, ethnicity, gender, education, self-image, and so forth. Groups do the same, based on their shared history and their organization's culture. As a result, individuals and groups frequently perceive and interpret the same event quite differently. Framing is the way an individual or group conceptualizes or defines a situation, issue, or problem based on their personal and group filters.

Reframing is a technique conflict managers use to help people look at things from a new frame of reference. Because you are detached from the conflict, you can see multiple perspectives and fresh ways to look at it. You can reframe the issues, giving the parties new ways of looking at things while reducing their risk of being seen as unsure, unclear, or indecisive. Reframing reactivates the parties' creativity and capacity for empathy, making them less defensive and more flexible.

"The spoken word belongs half to those who speak, and half to those who hear."

French proverb

You will find reframing useful in these situations:

- When the listener's emotional reaction to the speaker blocks his or her ability to hear the substance of the message

- When it is hard for the listener to see value in a message because of its emotional content or the speaker's stridency

- When people stubbornly believe the resolution of a conflict is an "either/or" situation

- When you want to articulate and test underlying interests that may exist in a stated position

There are three ways you, as conflict manager, can reframe a concept:

- Change the wording or delivery of what is said

- Alter the order or context of issues and ideas

- Identify pertinent issues or ideas not yet articulated

Suggestions for each of these approaches follow.

Change the wording

- Paraphrase what has been said, eliminating strident or blaming phrases while retaining the meaning of the statement. Change the emotion-laden statement "Mr. X never takes what I have to say seriously" to "It's very important to you that Mr. X seriously consider your ideas."

- Summarize what has been said by condensing it. Change "This office is a sty—there are papers everywhere, the wastebasket is overflowing, it's littered with filthy coffee cups growing new life forms. You can't even walk through here without tripping on garbage" to "You think it is important that an office be clean and orderly." This retains the statement's meaning without overwhelming the listener.

- Order issues in a more manageable sequence. Change "This task is too much! We need to completely redesign the program, develop a new budget, hire new staff, retrain old staff, figure out how to dump half the board of directors, get a new logo, find a new office space…" to "How about working on something that can be settled today, like a prioritized list of key tasks?"

- Break highly generalized statements into more specific bits of information. Change "The personnel policies in this organization are miserable" to "You would like to look at hiring practices, performance reviews, benefits, and what else?"

- Generalize by stating issues in broader terms. Change "This nonprofit has poor benefits, no harassment policies, no performance review procedures, and bad hiring practices" to "So you think that it is really important to review and revise the personnel practices in this organization."

- Broaden the meanings of terms used. Instead of generalizing from particulars as stated above, enlarge the meanings of words to give the parties more "mental room" for solutions. For example, change the title of the person who supports an executive director from secretary to administrative assistant, thereby suggesting more job responsibilities and growth potential.

- Have a different person communicate the message. Sometimes the parties' strong negative feelings about each other affects their ability to hear what each other is saying. The same message stated by you will be much more understandable and acceptable.

Alter the order or context of ideas

- Break large or complex issues into smaller issues. For example, break a conflict over a job performance evaluation into smaller issues that reflect the different aspects of the job listed in the position description.

- Reframe statements from positions to interests. When parties adamantly describe the conflict in terms of their positions, they are at a standoff. Reframe their positions as interests. For example, reframe a budget position from "We need an additional $50,000 to add a staff person" to "So to be effective you would like to add another staff member to the program." This shifts the argument from funding (a position) to a program need (an interest) and opens the option of finding staff support in some other way—staff sharing, internships, volunteer help, coordination with a similar agency, and so on.

- Change the context of the situation. Ask parties to think about a situation as though it were happening in another setting. For example, ask parties what they would do about the workplace conflict if it were happening at home, in another time period, or at another type of organization. This activity helps people get a new perspective on the issue.

- Identify common interests shared by the parties. People who focus on their differences easily overlook or undervalue their common interests. Reframe issues by identifying shared interests, such as the organization's mission and the people it serves.

- Minimize differences between people. Just as people in conflict forget about their common interests, they also magnify their differences. Point out how very close to a resolution the parties actually are. I heard about a divorce mediation in which the very last issue to be determined was how to divide the retirement income. The parties were only two hundred dollars apart, but each wanted the money. The mediator asked them, given all the work and tension involved in the divorce, which one thought it would be worth two hundred dollars to be done with the mediation and get their ex-spouse out of their life. They both volunteered to pay!

Identify unarticulated ideas

- Question or clarify the implied meaning of statements. I often call this "playing the dummy." At the conflict resolution table, you may be the only person who can afford to admit uncertainty about the issues in the conflict; the parties can't risk such vulnerability. Ask for clarification when statements seem vague or seem to have unstated implications. A "dumb" question can uncover an interest or concern that must be expressed to get the conflict resolution process moving. (One caveat: you must exude clarity and confidence about the conflict resolution process; never "play the dummy" about it.)

- Identify the positive value of something perceived as negative. People in conflict have a hard time seeing the bright side. You can help by offering your observations. For example, one organization was beset by conflict as it moved from the offices it had inhabited for a decade. The director reframed the move as an opportunity to lighten the load and focus on priorities, thus softening the work of the move.

- Raise relevant issues, facts, or ideas that have not been articulated. You are likely to see that information is missing and that relevant issues haven't been addressed. Bring these up so the parties can explore them.

- Suggest alternative motives or consequences for others' behaviors. Parties often attribute negative motives to each other, easily misunderstanding each other's real motives. If you believe this is happening, check it out during a private caucus rather than at the table. Be sure you reframe the motives in an exploratory way, using a phrase like "Might it be possible that the other party thinks that because…?" If you make declarative statements about the other party's motives, you may be viewed as their advocate.

As you can see, reframing can be done in many ways. Remember that the point of reframing is to refocus the parties' perspectives so that they can think more openly and creatively about the issues at hand. It is a powerful tool and a great stimulant to creative thinking in the conflict resolution process.

The following exercises will help you practice reframing.

EXERCISE

Reframing Issues

Reframe the following statements by rephrasing them using any of the techniques described previously. After trying one technique, try a different one on the same statement.

Example

Statement: "Management never listens to what we have to say."

Reframing:

1. "You feel that the communications between management and employees needs improvement."

2. "By 'listening,' do you mean that they do not solicit information, ideas, and opinions from employees, or that they don't respond to those ideas? Or is it something else?"

Exercise

"The development department must take the lead on this project."

1.

2.

(continued)

"That answer is too simplistic."

1.

2.

"We tried that before and it didn't work."

1.

2.

"The priority setting process is unfair to our program."

1.

2.

"That solution is not realistic."

1.

2.

"This line item in the budget seems very inflated."

1.

2.

"I can't get all of this done by then. This timeline is ridiculous."

1.

2.

Limiting Belittling and Blaming

There are two common types of statements found in conversation that set off people's "hot buttons" and tend to escalate conflicts: statements that belittle the other party and statements that place blame on the other party. Both add challenge to the conflict resolution process.

In belittling statements, one person states what they presume the other person thinks, feels, or does. Common examples of these statements are "You shouldn't feel that way," "So you think _____," and "Don't you know _____?!" These statements imply that the speaker thinks he or she knows better than the listener what the listener thinks, feels, or does. Statements like these make the listener feel both belittled and defensive.

The second type of statement ascribes blame. Placing blame distances the speaker from the problem and sets the onus of problem solving on the person being blamed. Common examples of blaming statements are "Because you _____," "Why can't you ever _____," and "They never _____." Blaming produces instant defensiveness and emotional response.

When one party blames or belittles another, you must quickly counter their statements. Reframing and restating the belittling or blaming comment may help. Another technique is to prevent belittling and blaming by beginning each conflict resolution meeting with ground rules for behavior. One of the ground rules is that parties must discuss the situation from their own perspectives. Sometimes conflict managers go so far as to suggest that parties begin all statements with "I think" or "I feel." This format prevents belittling and blaming because the sentence structure works against them.

In the thick of discussion, this guideline is frequently forgotten. When this happens and reminders of the agreed-upon ground rules don't stop a party from belittling or blaming, step in and request that the parties follow a structured format. Tell them that a belittling or blaming statement has been made and ask the speaker to rephrase their thoughts using the following formula:

I feel _____ when (you) _____ because _____.

For example, "I feel frustrated when you give me documents at 4:30 that have to be word processed by the end of the day because I have to pick up my child at day care at 5:30, and when I am late, I am fined extra by my child care provider."

This sentence structure makes the speaker "own" their concerns as their personal perspective, name their feelings, and explain why they feel as they do. It also removes accusatory or blaming words.

When people become used to expressing their ideas in this format, you can add a second statement that moves the conversation along further:

I will feel _____ if (you) _____ because _____.

For example, "I will be happy to type your documents if you give them to me earlier in the day because then I can meet your deadlines and still pick up my child on time."

This is a structured format for expressing ideas for solutions or changes. Its strength is that it states how a proposed action will affect the speaker and why. When parties show a great deal of resistance to each other's proposed solutions, stating their ideas in this format can make them more acceptable.

The following exercise will help you practice these techniques.

EXERCISE

Using Structured Statements to Limit Belittling and Blaming

To help others rephrase belittling or blaming statements in a more constructive format, you must try it yourself. Using the two formulas below, rephrase the following statements, first to express a concern and second to suggest a solution.

Formulas

Formula to express concerns:

1. I feel _____ when (you) _____ because _____.

Formula to suggest solutions:

2. I will feel _____ if (you) _____ because _____.

Example

No one ever answers the phones around here but me, and it's not my job.

1. I feel angry when people expect me to answer the phone because it's not part of my job description and I have other work to do.

2. I will feel relieved when you work with the other people in the office to arrange to get the phone answered without everyone relying on me.

Exercise phrases

1. These meetings are a waste of time.
2. We are never included in decision making that affects our work.
3. Why won't you listen to me?
4. This data doesn't make any sense.
5. You're late.
6. You are being overly sensitive.
7. Stop interrupting me.
8. You need to pull your weight around here.
9. The executive director doesn't have a clue.
10. There you go again.

Breaking Stalemates

When things look impossible in a conflict resolution process, there is often still hope. Here are two techniques that can help you break a stalemate: work backward and turn it upside down.

Work backward means taking the process back a few steps to see if something important has been missed or misunderstood. Turn it upside down means looking at the problem in new ways. Many of the upside-down methods are creative thinking techniques that help people break out of old thought patterns and test new ideas and assumptions. While upside-down methods are more radical and creative, working backward is usually the place to start when you have reached an impasse.

Working backward

Stalemates sometimes occur because important information is missing or misunderstood or because the conflict management process has moved too quickly for one or all of the parties. In either case, it is time to move backward. Don't be disheartened; moving backward does not mean that you need to invest the same amount of time in the process that you already have. Rather, it means going back in an abbreviated way to review and revisit what has already been said and done. This frequently brings to light conditions that led to the deadlock—missing information, absent parties, unidentified interests, unacknowledged feelings, different understandings, concerns about losing face, or unfounded assumptions.

Often the missing information is crucial to one party, but they have been unwilling to make it known to the other party. You can use a caucus to explore the hidden obstructions privately. When you learn what the blockage is, you and the party can agree on ways to bring it to light so the process can move forward. Sometimes it's appropriate for the conflict manager to carry the message (only with the party's approval, of course), either by raising it at the table or in caucus with the other party.

Here are some tips for working backward:

- Go back to people's understanding of the problem and their commitment to resolving it—their original agreement to work in a conflict resolution process. To do this, revisit their motives for resolving the conflict, the benefits they hope to gain, and their hopes for their future working relationship and conditions. The goal is to have them either recommit to working through the conflict together or to uncover any serious doubts or assumptions that might be causing the stalemate.

- Go back to each person's description of the situation. Was information missed in the first telling? Do you or the parties need to collect information from others in order to proceed? Does information that seemed unimportant suddenly have more significance? Are there unspoken interests? Have expressed or implied emotions or concerns about the interpersonal relationship been adequately addressed? Do you sense gaps in information or in the sequence of events as they have been described? If so, is a party intentionally omitting information, possibly because it is something he or she is unwilling to say in the presence of the other party? This situation might call for a caucus to discover what is being withheld and why.

- Check the definitions everyone is using. What does each party mean by "fair" or other value-laden words? Are both parties defining the issues in the same way? Frequently a stalemate is caused by people using the same words, but not meaning the same thing. Can you reframe the issues or definitions so that the parties can see the issue from both their perspectives? Can you present an entirely different perspective to help them look at the issue in a new way?

- Check out people's interests. It is common for people not to recognize their own interests or for important new ones to emerge during the conflict resolution process. Do you sense an implied interest that the parties have not recognized? Check out this possibility with the parties. A hidden or unrecognized interest often creates a stalemate.

- Review the options on the table. Without asking for commitment from either party, review the possible options for resolution and test their strengths and weaknesses. People may reject a viable option because of misunderstandings, judgment clouded by emotion, or the inability to visualize its implementation. Explore possibilities, tinker with the options, and create new ones. Sometimes suggesting extreme solutions can jar people into creativity or to a more realistic assessment of the options already on the table.

- Use caucuses to discover the root of the impasse. Call a caucus to ask what each party thinks is creating the impasse and what they would need to move ahead. You can also explore each party's expectations. Are they feasible and realistic? Test options that may not have been raised at the table. Check with the parties about their best and worst alternatives to a negotiated agreement by discussing best and worst possible outcomes of cutting off the conflict resolution process.

- Use Rogerian Dialogue to help parties hear and acknowledge each other. Psychologist Carl Rogers developed this structured communication technique almost forty years ago. It is very useful in highly emotional conflicts, because it reduces the "mental noise" going on in the parties' brains. This noise is made up of memories, rebuttals, associations, and other related or unrelated thoughts. Rogerian Dialogue requires a lot of concentration and therefore reduces the mental noise and increases understanding.

Rogerian Dialogue feels artificial and awkward at first. Acknowledge this and ask the parties to play along—otherwise, people may refuse to participate. First have one party explain their idea or issue. The second party then repeats their understanding of the statement in their own words. The first party either agrees that the second party fully and accurately understood and restated what was first said, or restates and clarifies the meaning of their original remarks. The second party, again in their own words, restates the meaning until the first party confirms that his or her ideas have been understood and restated accurately. The parties then continue their conversation, using this confirmation and clarification process alternately.

Usually, Rogerian Dialogue de-escalates emotions and forces listening. The speaker's sense of being genuinely heard defuses considerable frustration and anger.

Turn the conflict upside down

Ever capsize a boat, even a small one? You get a dramatically different view. You also gain a fresh appreciation of the benefits of the boat itself. The techniques that follow show you how to "capsize" a conflict, but with beneficial results. Each technique turns the issues upside down, to see if looking at them differently will reveal the situation from a fresh, more creative vantage.

> **Figure 6. How Rogerian Dialogue works**
>
> Party A: Explains the issue from his or her perspective
>
> Party B: Restates his or her understanding of Party A's statements
>
> Party A: Either confirms that Party B is correct or restates the issue to correct misunderstood information
>
> Party B: Restates Party A's corrections to information in his or her own words
>
> Party A: Confirms (or corrects again)
>
> When Party A feels that Party B has fully and correctly restated what was said, the parties reverse roles. Party B states his or her issues, Party A restates, and Party B confirms or corrects.
>
> It seems like this could go on forever, but it doesn't. Bit by bit, as people sense the other party is hearing them, emotions are defused, and normal dialogue takes over. Parties frequently let you know when the structured dialogue is no longer needed.

- Run a role play in which the parties assume each other's roles. Some people have great difficulty role-playing, but when people are willing, this technique can help them get new ideas. To role-play, each party states the issues and possible resolutions from the other party's perspective. People will need time to think this through; it is not easy to jump to the other side of an argument when you have an investment in your own. However, a walk in the other guy's shoes, so to speak, helps parties develop much more empathy for each other. After switching back to their own shoes, they can frequently find ways to address each other's concerns.

- Reverse the issue to bring up new and different solutions. Use this creative problem-solving technique when people run out of ideas. Whatever the problem, the parties work on its opposite—identifying issues and seeking solutions. If the real issue is having too few volunteers, the parties discuss issues raised by having too many volunteers and solutions for those issues.

- Ask each party to divide the resource pie so that they would be satisfied receiving any portion. Try this technique when the issues are over the "fair" division of resources. This technique is used by some families as follows: when treats are to be shared, one sibling cuts the item and the others pick first. This approach encourages the sibling who divides the portions to be fair to all siblings. To use this technique, assign each party the task of dividing the resources so that they would be satisfied with any portion. All parties make what they believe is a fair division of the resources and share their plans for division with the others.

Occasionally, the parties simply choose one of the plans and use it for resolution. But more commonly parties use the plans to craft a modified resolution. The technique has two benefits beyond helping people divide resources. First, they are often pleased and surprised to see the other party being "fair." Second, when making the division, parties often demonstrate sensitivity to the needs expressed by the others. These demonstrations of fairness and sensitivity help parties rebuild rapport that may have eroded during the conflict.

In this chapter you've learned many skills for finessing the fine points of conflict resolution. With practice, you should be able to untangle many a knotty conflict. But the seas are full of mysteries. Some day, you'll venture into the Bermuda Triangle—that spot infamous for the disappearance of ships large and small. Help is available, though. In the next chapter, you'll learn skills for handling some of the more unusual conflicts that await you.

CHAPTER FOUR

The Bermuda Triangle
Conflicts That Require Special Handling

YOU MAY ENCOUNTER special types of conflict that require processes other than those described previously. Two types of special conflict exist: ones that seem to be irresolvable and ones that involve groups like boards, volunteers, and funders, whose affiliations with the organization are different from those of staff or vendors. You may also encounter special situations, such as harassment, discrimination, conflicts involving vulnerable people, and illegal activities, for which there are prescribed regulations. This chapter will show you how to handle all these situations and will also guide you in finding and selecting outside help with conflict resolution, if you need it.

Standing Waves: How and Why People Remain in Conflict

In rivers there is a phenomenon called standing waves. Because of the forces moving the water and the shape of the riverbed, these waves appear to stand still. Kayakers like to play in standing waves, physicists like to create them in experiments—and surprisingly, people sometimes like to "wallow" in the standing waves of conflict.

People often choose to maintain a conflict because it fulfills needs that are more important to them than relief from the stress of conflict. Some reasons why people maintain conflicts include:

- The fear of losing control of something
- Difficulty admitting mistakes or a fear of making mistakes
- A competitive worldview coupled with a fear of losing
- A fear of showing one's true feelings or needs
- Maintenance of a relationship using conflict as a vehicle

For people caught in these fears and emotions, remaining in a conflict may be preferable to resolving it. If you're alert to common tactics used to sustain a conflict, you may be able to break through the impasse. Following are some standard standing waves of conflict:

The old sea dog: Always unearthing bones of the past

An old sea dog is the person who digs up every past "wrong" no matter how old it is or whether it is related to the current conflict. The old bones seem to overwhelm all efforts to resolve the conflict. If you notice that someone is dwelling on old issues rather than resolving the current conflict, you might consider whether you are working with an old sea dog.

In order to get a conflict resolved with an old sea dog you must unearth the person's underlying concerns. Do this, and you'll bury many of the bones once and for all.

Here's an example of an old sea dog at work. Four support staff came to me with a conflict over summer vacation scheduling. During the discussion one person raised issues of poor workload distribution, difficulty covering other people's absences, the overall quality of the group's work, and so on. Many of the examples were events that had happened months, even years, before. For some time, we all discussed ways to resolve these problems since we recognized that some of them had merit. However, the complaining person found all suggested solutions unacceptable and kept asking for a reorganization of the support staff. By the end of the meeting the issue of vacation scheduling was still unresolved and the situation seemed hopelessly mired.

After the meeting, the dissatisfied person and I met privately. I sensed that there was more to her concerns than she had divulged. In our conversation, she aired her views of the deficiencies of the other support staff's work and said she felt undervalued. This feeling was what was driving her to stall the process. She had worked at the agency for several years and wanted to move into an administrative position. Once I understood this I agreed to steps that would help her develop her administrative skills.

The next meeting with the support staff was a cakewalk. We solved the vacation scheduling issue quickly and went on to discuss and resolve a number of other issues. Our work was astonishingly quick and painless. All of us were amazed given the length and tension in our previous meeting.

In hindsight I saw why the nay-saying person had wanted to keep the conflict unresolved. Maintaining the scheduling conflict allowed her to raise "concerns" about the organization of the secretarial pool and the quality of the work. Her call for reorganizing the pool was a bid to advance her career. She did not want to lose this forum to position herself as the most skilled person on the support staff. Once I had unearthed her true interests, we were able to resolve the conflict and deal with her wishes for recognition and career advancement.

The admiral: Winning is who I am

Highly competitive people sometimes choose to maintain a conflict rather than risk losing what they view as a competition. In their win/lose worldview, they see winning as gaining or retaining power and losing as forfeiting power. If a conflict is not winnable a highly competitive person might prefer to continue it rather than view themselves as losing.

If you're working with an admiral in conflict your challenge is helping her or him view the conflict as other than a personal win or loss. Avoid the use of words common to competition, such as winner, loser, superior, inferior, prize, defeat, and so forth, when describing the conflict or possible solutions. Develop solutions that allow the admiral to gain or retain his or her personal power. Here's an example of an admiral whose insistence on winning eventually cost him dearly.

A nonprofit executive was in conflict with his board of directors. The executive had previous training as an attorney, a profession that often emphasizes the win/lose worldview. For the first time in his career in the organization, he had received a performance appraisal that indicated a need for improvement in his human resources management practices. As a result, he received only a cost-of-living increase, not the merit pay increase he had anticipated. The board asked him to get training in some of his deficient management areas. He refused, talked of suing the board for slander, proposed an injunction against the board chair, and engaged in activities that created divisiveness among board members. This continued for several years, accompanied by rapid board turnover and negative relations between the organization's board and staff.

The executive was a highly competitive individual who had never received anything less than a superior performance appraisal. Although the proposed training course he was to take was one executives of other nonprofit organizations often sought, he equated taking the training with losing. Rather than view himself as a loser, he created and maintained turmoil. In the end, he lost—his job.

"Our tempers are what get us into trouble. Our pride is what keeps us in it."

Mark Twain,
American humorist

The water roiler: Keeping the water stirred to confuse the issues

Some people do not wish to acknowledge they are involved in a conflict at all. In an effort to avoid conflict, they say one thing and do another, sending mixed messages. This behavior may mask a fear of displaying their true concerns or feelings. While the water roiler hopes to avoid conflict, their behavior actually escalates the frustrations and anger of others involved in the conflict. Frequently the roiler will repeatedly state there is no problem or will agree to most anything, but not carry it out.

The roiler may also direct subtle digs or slights at others in the conflict. His or her words, gestures, posture, or tone of voice may not match the substance of what he or she is saying, confusing people on the receiving end. Asking the roiler to rephrase or explain their statement will sometimes clarify their real meaning. You can handle digs in the same way.

Because water roilers are acting in fear, you must assure them they will be safe in the conflict resolution process. By making sure that communications between people in the conflict are respectful and honest and by encouraging the use of active listening skills, you can create an environment in which a roiler may risk divulging his or her genuine concerns and feelings.

Here is a story of a water roiler at work. A group of fifteen adult students in a nonprofit management class were given the choice of getting individual grades or a group grade for a group assignment. However, the group had to reach consensus on which type of grade they preferred. During numerous protracted discussions about grading, one student frequently claimed that she was flexible about the issue, but also mentioned that she preferred receiving an individual grade. During the discussions, she repeated her statement about flexibility, but never changed her position about receiving an individual grade. She often sat pushed back from the table with arms crossed. As she reminded people of her flexibility, her body language and tone made it clear that she was anything but flexible. The class discussed the grade issue for the entire term. At one point, the group had almost decided to have a shared grade, except for the "flexible" student. The group never reached consensus, and the key reason was the flexible person's inflexibility.

The bickerers: Conflicts keep us together

When I first learned that people sometimes maintain a conflict to preserve a relationship I could not believe it. But I had it brought home to me loud and clear by my own children, who frequently argued over insubstantial matters. The noise and tone of their conflicts annoyed my husband and me. One day, when her brother was away from home, my daughter said to me, "I miss arguing with Ethan."

"Why?" I asked.

"It's our way of being together," she said. I suddenly saw that people in a relationship sometimes create a conflict so that they can continue to relate. The way to end these conflicts is to replace them with a shared interest or concern. This creates a bond that replaces bickering.

Bickering is most common as a tool to maintain relationships. You'll note it in the nonprofit environment among colleagues who have different work or communication styles. Continual bickering about the differences can actually be a part of their working relationship.

The process maven: No one can do it right

A group of people discussing an issue are about to reach an agreement. Suddenly, someone in the group raises concerns about the process used to come to the decision. This person is probably a process maven. His or her concerns may be about the process used to reach agreement, the processes used to collect information, or the information itself. Process questions are legitimate, but if someone raises them regularly with the effect of stalling or stalemating an agreement, you may be faced with a process maven.

People use this technique for several reasons. Sometimes the person disagrees with the decision but doesn't care to state their real reason for disagreeing. In other cases they fear or don't want the responsibility that the agreement might produce. And sometimes they want to be viewed as an expert or leader, but have not been recognized by the group as such.

Though this tactic is probably age-old, it seems to have gained new life as organizations increasingly use teams and engage in more collaborations—and it is especially prevalent in nonprofit organizations. Group decision-making is ripe with opportunities for process mavens. The following story is typical of the work of a process maven.

A team in a nonprofit organization was assigned to develop a process for evaluating program effectiveness. The work was significant to the organization; it was to be used to improve programming, and some of the data was to be shared with current and future funders. The team included people with experience designing evaluations as well as program staff whose programs would be evaluated. Team members were compatible and seemed committed to the task.

Though they generated many ideas for an effective evaluation process, they never could agree on a design. Each time they seemed close to agreement, one or two members always found fault with some aspect of the process. Other team members were wildly frustrated because their work on this important project seemed hopelessly stalled. The team leader finally discussed the situation with the organization's executive, who decided to talk informally with team members to discover what was going on.

She uncovered two issues that thwarted the team's ability to complete their task. One team member, who held a Ph.D., thought that because of his expertise in research, he should have been assigned the role of team leader. Another team member, one of the program managers, was worried that the program she ran, which dealt with youths whom every other program had given up on, would look poor in any evaluation. Both people had been using the process maven technique to stall or end the project because of their individual concerns. The executive assured the Ph.D. team member that he would lead a team on a big upcoming project. This enabled him to accept the team's work. The worried program manager was tougher. The team eventually tailored the evaluation process to reflect the goals established by her program.

Board Conflicts

As I mentioned in the first chapter, board conflicts are among the most challenging conflicts a nonprofit executive faces. They generally come in two forms—conflicts among board members and conflicts between the board and professional management of the organization, either the executive or the staff. Both of these difficult situations require special consideration.

It is not uncommon for half the membership of a board to resign or just drift away from a board as a significant conflict unfolds. This loss of valuable leadership and talent drains the nonprofit's resources.

Conflict among Board Members

I have yet to hear an executive director who relishes board conflicts. Though most executives value board members' constructive disagreements about what is best for the organization, they fear the times when these disagreements become destructive. Many board members also dislike conflicts, so much so that they frequently abdicate their board responsibilities rather than deal with them.

A recent study of the members of over fifty boards in Minnesota found that most people join boards to "network, make friends, and do good." The study also reported that avoiding conflict is the most common reason for members' resignations. It is not uncommon for half the membership of a board to resign or just drift away from a board as a significant conflict unfolds.[9] This loss of valuable leadership and talent drains the nonprofit's resources. Time and money must be spent to solicit, orient, and bring new board members up to speed. In addition, resigning board members may cost the organization in contributions and reputation. For these reasons, it's imperative that you both manage the conflict to a resolution and keep as many board members as possible committed to your organization.

Facilitating a conflict among board members holds a real danger for an executive. He or she frequently ends up caught in the choppy waters between warring bosses—set up to sink no matter what the outcome. In a board conflict, it is nearly impossible for an executive to maintain each board member's belief in his or her

---

[9] Bryant, Nancy L. "MAP Board Inventory Shows: The Connection Is the Key to a Positive Board Experience." Minneapolis: University of St. Thomas, MAP Points Sept. 1994.

impartiality. Some board members will inevitably believe that the executive is somehow manipulating the situation or come to view him or her as an ally of the opposing party. True or not, these beliefs will erode the board's trust and confidence in the executive—the key factors for a successful working relationship between an executive and board.

Even if you have strong ideas about the issues dividing a board, it is wise to let the board chair take the lead in resolving conflicts within the board. After all, managing the board is the chair's job. Unfortunately, many chairs do not understand or accept the full scope of their responsibilities. And many would rather not deal with conflict even when they understand that it is their role.

The emotional element in board conflicts

One factor that contributes to the challenge of handling board conflicts is the emotional rancor that often occurs. A discussion that begins as a difference in members' views on a business issue can quickly become intense and personal. Some board members make personal attacks or embarrass others as they argue their points. The negative feelings created by public embarrassment perpetuate the dispute even when the conflict can be settled easily.

When exchanges get negative and personal, two things happen. The board members in conflict have increasing difficulty communicating constructively, and uninvolved board members become increasingly uncomfortable watching the negative exchanges. After a negative exchange at a meeting, a skilled chair will encourage the parties to resolve their issues away from the boardroom. On boards, as in other group settings, small conflicts left unresolved tend to simmer into a rich stew of resentment. Early intervention by the board chair can prevent this.

One of the most frequently used strategies in board conflicts is private meetings. This is not done to keep the board conflict a secret but for the comfort of both the disputing parties and the uninvolved board members. To conduct a private meeting, the board chair can use shuttle diplomacy, speaking privately with individual board members. Also, he or she can bring a limited number of disagreeing members together privately for a facilitated discussion outside of the boardroom. This can be especially helpful when a board conflict is among only a few of the board members. However, the number of members a chair can convene without the meeting becoming an official board meeting is affected by the organization's quorum stipulations. If the number of people in the conflict constitutes a quorum, it is a formal meeting of the board and all members should be invited to attend. If uninvolved members know the meeting topic, they can choose whether to attend, but they should not be excluded.

When a conflict that includes loss of face (the result of being belittled or shamed) erupts in a board meeting and is then resolved privately, be sure that the noninvolved members who witnessed the confrontation know that it has been resolved. Otherwise, they may be confused or believe that important decisions are being made behind their backs. The board chair can simply state that the problems between the disagreeing members have been cleared up.

Conflict resolution resources

I stated earlier that the best way for an executive director to manage conflict within a board is to turn it over to the board chair. The conflict management process and techniques in this book also work for board leaders. So in addition to offering your own knowledge of conflict management, provide this book as a resource.

Don't be surprised to find board leaders uncomfortable with conflict and its management. Remember, few people enjoy or expect to have to resolve conflict as their contribution to the work of your organization. The power relationship between an executive and the board, as well as the impossibility of the executive being perceived as neutral, argue strongly against the executive serving as the conflict manager.

If you have a board chair who will accept the conflict manager role, willingly or reluctantly, thank your lucky stars. Support the chair by coaching him or her on conflict analysis, process design, and other skills. No matter how much analysis or coaching you provide, however, the board chair must take the lead in managing the conflict.

If your board chair, even with your support and coaching, is unwilling or unable to manage the conflict, you might seek another leader. A vice chair might fill this role, although members may ask why the chair is not managing the conflict. This can undermine the chair's authority, which you want to avoid. A highly respected past board chair or board member can be a good choice. Whoever you choose, the person should have conflict management skills, be well regarded by all the parties, be viewed as impartial toward the parties and be objective about the issues.

If neither current nor past board leaders are willing or able to manage the conflict, consider using a skilled mediator. For information on finding and choosing a mediator, see Finding External Help with Conflict Resolution, pages 139-142.

Conflict between Board and Executive or Staff

Conflicts between the executive or other staff and the board are extremely delicate. First, a significant power imbalance exists, since the board is the executive's employer. Second, the executive is the bridge between the board and staff and must understand and represent these groups' differing viewpoints to each other. This can be very delicate and precarious.

An executive can wind up in conflict with the board in three ways: When staff conflict is brought to the board; when direct conflict exists between the executive

The power relationship between an executive and the board, as well as the impossibility of the executive being perceived as neutral, argue strongly against the executive serving as the conflict manager.

and some or all of the board members; and when a staff person makes an end run, bypassing the executive and bringing an issue directly to the board.

When staff conflict is brought to the board

A staff conflict brought before the board can ensnare the executive, causing him or her to lose the board's confidence. To the board, the executive represents staff leadership, and is responsible for maintaining staff productivity and harmony. Given this, board members tend to regard staff conflicts brought to them as an indication of a deficiency in the executive's management skills. Board members often resent having to manage staff conflicts—after all, they did not donate their leisure time to resolve staff battles.

Even so, the board should step in when efforts to resolve a conflict at the staff level have not succeeded. When you bring a staff conflict to the board, outline the nature of the problem and explain the process you want to board to use. If the issue requires confidentiality, explain the organization's obligation to maintain confidentiality.

Often the board chair or personnel committee assume the role of hearing and resolving staff conflicts that come before the board. If your organization's bylaws or the charters of your subcommittees authorize the personnel or executive committee to handle conflicts, activate one of these committees. If not, I suggest that you encourage the board to delegate the task to one of these two committees. There are three reasons for this. First, the use of a subcommittee gives the organization two chances for internal conflict resolution before turning to an outside agency—first through the subcommittee, and then through the full board if necessary. Second, the use of a subcommittee contains the information about the conflict, keeping it more confidential. Finally, the use of a subcommittee frees the rest of the board to attend to the organization's other important business.

The subcommittee conflict resolution process is much like the process I described in Chapter Two; the subcommittee hears from all the parties and helps generate and test potential solutions. However, the subcommittee also serves as arbitrator, developing a resolution it believes is best for the organization and the parties in conflict. Depending on the bylaws or charter of the subcommittee, the decision can either stand as decided or may need to be ratified by the entire board. If the people in the conflict are still unsatisfied, they can turn to the full board for a hearing before moving on to external assistance.

One caveat: If a conflict is brought to the board and delegated to a subcommittee, all board members must understand the benefits of having a subcommittee handle the conflict. If uninvolved board members don't fully understand why it is prudent that only a few board members know the full details of the conflict, they can feel excluded. Also, the full board should be told the outcome of the conflict (not the details) and its implications for the organization.

When board and executive are in direct conflict

When an executive director is in serious direct conflict with the board, he or she usually "loses" and may resign or be fired. Occasionally the whole board resigns and the executive establishes a new board that supports him or her. In either case, the organization usually loses momentum, continuity, expertise, and leadership. Additionally, a conflict resolved in this way is likely to cost the organization money, the confidence of its staff, and its good name—perhaps its most valuable asset.

Few such conflicts erupt suddenly. Usually they are preceded by smaller conflicts that, if not handled well, erode the confidence or trust between the board and the executive. Handling small conflicts when they occur is important because once a direct conflict breaks out between board and executive, it is extremely difficult to resolve.

When a significant conflict develops between the executive and the board, rapid action and professional help are called for. Clearly an executive cannot manage a significant conflict in which he or she is a party. Neither can the board chair. In this case an external resource is the best option. Some choices include

- A mediator
- An organizational consultant with conflict management skills
- The organization's previous board chair, executive, or similar leader with conflict management skills

When considering these resources, be sure that they will be viewed as unbiased by all parties.

I wish I could be optimistic about resolving conflicts between the executive and board. In my experience, however, neither the executive nor board leader (more frequently the board) have been eager to use a conflict resolution process. Instead the conflict quickly becomes a battle of wills and wiles. I believe nonprofit leaders hesitate to use conflict resolution processes in board-executive conflicts because people's identities are threatened and so much is at stake. The executive's livelihood, career, and professional reputation are threatened, and board members' identities as stewards with the ultimate authority in the organization are at risk. The two sides quickly become locked in a war of egos and wills.

This is precisely the type of situation where a neutral outsider can help, but nonprofit leaders need to have enough knowledge about and confidence in the conflict resolution process—in advance of needing it—to know that the process can only help, not hurt, their situation.

If the board and executive know about conflict resolution processes and, for the sake of the organization, are willing to try to mediate their conflict, they must first work together to select a mediator. Page 65 has a list of criteria for selecting a mediator. In this situation the key criterion is that the person be viewed as neutral—someone all the parties already know and trust equally or someone previously unknown to the board and executive.

Nonprofit leaders need to have enough knowledge about and confidence in the conflict resolution process— in advance of needing it— to know that the process can only help, not hurt, their situation.

When staff makes an end run

A staff end run can have serious repercussions, as this story shows. An organization I had direct experience with had a loose sick leave policy, with no limits on the number of sick leave hours an employee could use. Instead, the director granted sick leave at her discretion. The director originally recommended and liked the latitude of this policy until a newer staff member began taking excessive numbers of sick days. Morale plummeted among the other staff, who had to cover for their "sick" colleague. The director asked the board's personnel committee to develop a clearer sick leave policy. They did this and brought their recommendation to the board for approval.

In the meantime, the staff person who overused sick leave did an end run. She knew two board members and talked them into disapproving the policy. When the board reviewed the personnel committee's work, the two members objected, citing that the proposed policy was punitive toward the staff person who had contacted them. The members of the personnel committee were frustrated, since neither of these board members had given the committee requested input while they were writing the policy. Things got personal and harsh words flew around the board table. After trying at several meetings to deal with the issue, the board—now severely divided—ultimately tabled the question and never picked it up again.

Subsequently, the executive director felt betrayed by her board, the board had conflicts over other issues, and staff became increasingly unhappy about covering for the "sick" person. The issue and the conflicts it generated contributed to high staff turnover and the resignation of the director.

What could the organization have done differently? Perhaps most important, both new employees and board members needed to be told during orientation that the executive director is the point person for the board of directors. In some larger organizations, staff are not allowed to communicate with board members. In smaller and more informal organizations, there is often no such restriction—but in all cases, the policy should be to keep the executive director informed of any interactions with board members.

When an end run occurs, the executive needs to talk with the board members and the staff involved about the board-staff communications policy. A naïve staff person is easily educated, but one who is unwilling to follow protocol is another matter. Staff who understand the way executives work with the board generally make end runs when they feel the executive isn't supporting them and believe all other avenues are closed. Because end runs are risky and put them in direct conflict with the executive, a staff person has to be very desperate or angry to take the chance. In general, this means the staff person and the executive are probably involved in an unresolved conflict. It's imperative to work through the conflict that motivated the staff member to risk an end run. Such a conflict will likely require the assistance of a mediator for resolution.

Both new employees and board members need to be told during orientation that the executive director is the point person for the board of directors.

It is also important to remind the staff person about expectations that he or she follow the organization's communication policy—and to discuss the consequences of disregarding the policy. This discussion should be documented. Disciplinary action (based on the written personnel policy) may be required, but it should be used sparingly because the goal is to set a positive tone for settling the dispute, not to fuel the fire.

It's equally imperative to immediately talk with the board members who were involved in the end run—about the substance of the concern raised by the staff member, how you are handling the conflict, and the problems created by not following existing communication policies. Don't be surprised if they are unaware of the policy or the reasons it exists.

Your first goal is to get the issue off the board table until you and the staff person have made every effort to work through the conflict. Depending on your board's policies and on their involvement in the conflict, you may then have to bring the resolution before the board for approval. Your second goal is to regain the trust of the board members involved. Honest communication is the best route to rebuilding their confidence. If your efforts to resolve the conflict fail, you should be the person to bring the conflict to the board.

Given the inevitability of conflict in nonprofits, your board members need to know how to have constructive conflicts. You are the person who must help them better understand conflict and develop ways to disagree constructively—before serious conflicts erupt. Healthy conflict on a board can stimulate creativity and strengthen the organization. Training your board in the processes of healthy conflict is always a worthwhile investment of the organization's resources.

Conflicts with Funders

Many times nonprofits feel like their hands are tied when they find themselves in conflict with an agency or individual that funds them. Nonprofits complain that the funders have all the power. Indeed there is a power imbalance; funders have resource power over nonprofits. But the relationship between funder and nonprofit is not as out of balance as one might think. Funders and nonprofits are interdependent and work within a tight community in which their organizations' good names are critical elements. To be viewed as effective, both must retain the public's trust and be recognized for their contributions to the community.

Unresolved conflicts between funders and nonprofits jeopardize both organizations' assets. In the nonprofit community, as in any other industry, the power of informal networks is significant. Neither funders nor nonprofits can afford negative information on the grapevine.

When there has been a conflict, it is in the best interest of the nonprofit to rebuild a relationship with the funder because future funding is always possible. Reconciliation is also in the funder's interest because funders depend on nonprofits to turn their dollars into good works. The funder's reputation depends on the nonprofit's wise use of the funder's investment.

There are generally three types of conflicts between nonprofits and funders: resource allocation conflicts, data collection and reporting conflicts, and relationship conflicts.

Resource allocation conflicts

The most common conflict between a nonprofit and a funder is over resource allocations. As a nonprofit leader, you are passionate about your mission and organization, and you may be stunned when a funder does not share your sense of urgency and pride. But to the funder your organization is one of many worthy organizations and causes, and your requests must be prioritized to fit the resources available. The funder's annual report stating that it can fund only one in five or ten of its annual requests may seem a vague abstraction. Many times funders turn down requests from worthy nonprofits because there just are not enough funds.

Ultimately a funder decides among worthy proposals based on how it balances its priorities. The funding board may take into account previous funding decisions, the forceful ideas of an influential board member, and the unconscious preferences or biases of board members. Funding allocation is a group-process decision, and it is not always explainable. The same group of people could have made a different decision on a different day. Though the funder's program officers can give you insights into the funder's priorities and decision-making process, they may not be able to fully explain the funder's decisions.

What should you do when you have a conflict with a funder over their decision not to give you a grant? Understand that the people making the decisions are doing their best to be thoughtful, prudent, and purposeful. Blow off some steam, and then contact the funder's program officer and ask for advice. Don't ask for information about the particular decision not to fund your program, as this puts the program officer in a difficult position. Ask how to be successful with the funder with a future proposal. Program officers serve both as bridges and buffers between the funding board and the applicants. Many make funding recommendations to their boards, but these recommendations may not always be honored.

Figure 7. Funders' Principles for Communication with Grant Seekers

The Council on Foundations, a national membership association of grantmaking foundations, has developed principles for its member organizations. They state that members should treat grant seekers with respect and candor and disclose their procedures and policies to grant seekers and the public. Some local or regional councils have adopted similar policies, often with more detailed guidelines. The principles are designed to be adopted by foundations' boards and used as a self-governing tool. Having a copy of the principles can help you if a problem arises between your organization and a funder.

Principles and Practices for Effective Grant Making are available from the Council on Foundations, 1828 L St. NW, Washington, DC 20036. You might also request the principles of the regional associations for areas in which your nonprofit works. A list of those associations is available from the Forum of Regional Associations of Grantmakers, also at the address above.

Use the situation as an opportunity to build a relationship for the future. Seek advice about how the denied proposal might have been strengthened in form or content. Ask about the interests and priorities of the funder and how your organization's work might fit with their goals. Many foundation program officers act as advocates, helping nonprofits make a strong case to their foundation. Because they read so many different proposals and know how nonprofit organizations work, their insights can be extremely useful.

View this process of clarification as the first step in developing your next request to the funder. Seek information in a professional manner that builds confidence and respect for you and your organization. Remember that even if you don't plan to solicit funds from this funder again, the world of philanthropy is small. Funders contact others about organizations when researching proposals, and program officers move from one philanthropic organization to another throughout their careers.

Data collection and reporting conflicts

Data collection and reporting can be contentious issues between nonprofits and government or large community-based funders. Nonprofits with limited staffs and resources often find the amount of data requested and the reporting formats required are onerous. In such conflicts, it is essential for each party to understand the interests of the other. The nonprofit must understand how the funder plans to use the data, and the funder must understand the nonprofit's limited resources for data collection.

Though some nonprofits often don't see the value in data reporting, funders need data that show whoever provides them money (government or contributors) that their gifts are well used. Reports and data are often used for this purpose. However, funders sometimes develop data and reporting requirements with too little thought about how the data will be used. (Collecting data because it is "interesting" is a common pitfall.) Clarifying the uses for data often helps parties figure out which data are valuable, as well as how to collect and report data in ways that save time and resources—and even result in improved service delivery.

Most of the conflict resolution techniques discussed earlier apply to this sort of conflict. Even if no conflict manager facilitates the discussion, identifying interests, reframing issues, and applying constructive communication skills can lead to a constructive resolution. If necessary and if both parties agree, a conflict manager or mediator can facilitate discussions.

Although data and reports are the substantive issues under discussion, it's important to consider the parties' relationship needs. If relations are not handled well, requirements for reports and data can become the basis of a power struggle, to the detriment of both parties.

Relationship conflicts

On rare occasions a funding agency's staff behaves disrespectfully to the staff or board of a nonprofit seeking the funder's support. If the conflict is harassing or discriminatory, the nonprofit needs to report the behavior to the funding agency's management. If the funder is unresponsive, the person can take their claim to responsible government agencies.

More commonly, inappropriate behavior isn't as severe as harassment or discrimination, but it is still of a nature that requires reporting to the funding institution. Report your concerns either directly to the staff person involved or to that person's manager, using your judgment about which is more appropriate. If you are worried about possible reprisal, say so. Disrespectful or unresponsive behavior by staff tarnish the funder's reputation in the community. If working on a conflict with the staff person in question feels too threatening, you might suggest that his or her manager or another person who is mutually respected facilitate the meeting.

Conflicts Involving Volunteers

Distinctions between paid staff and volunteers are disappearing. Nonprofits are now encouraged to treat volunteers much like paid staff, giving them position descriptions, training, performance appraisals, and recognition. In addition, nonprofits are legally responsible for the behavior of all their staff, paid and volunteer, when they are doing the work of the organization. Issues of harassment, maltreatment, and discrimination apply to volunteers and paid staff alike. When managing a conflict involving a volunteer, look for circumstances such as harassment or abuse that require special action and handle them as you would with paid staff to avoid putting your organization at risk.[10]

Though you will use much the same conflict management process with volunteers as with paid staff, there are two differences to keep in mind. First, volunteering is an exchange and second, volunteers hold informal power.

Volunteering is an exchange

Though unpaid, volunteers receive many things in exchange for their work:

- Connections with other people
- Feeling valued
- Knowledge and skills for use in future paid positions
- The means to move into a different sector of the economy or gain experience in a new field when changing careers
- The opportunity to get work experience and demonstrate work readiness

All or any of these motivations might be a benefit in the exchange between the volunteer and the organization. Understanding the specific benefit to the volunteer can often give you clues to the interests that underlie a conflict between a volunteer and a nonprofit.

Volunteers hold informal power

Some volunteers carry significant informal power. A volunteer may have high status in the community, be a donor to the organization, or have family or friends among the staff, board, or funders. Volunteers who have been with the organization a long time may hold formal power if they manage other volunteers, budgets, or other resources. When managing a conflict, consider the informal and formal power a volunteer holds.

A volunteer who is involved in a conflict is not necessarily a "difficult" volunteer, although some of the books about volunteers and conflict use this term.[11] Conflict involving a volunteer can be of any type already described. The best form of volunteer conflict management is prevention derived from clear volunteer policies, so establish some policies and procedures for volunteers in advance of a conflict or problem. Here are the key points to include in an organization's volunteer policies:

- Position descriptions and performance standards for each volunteer position.

- A volunteer performance evaluation.

- A statement expressing the organization's ability to change a volunteer's duties, transfer him or her, or end the relationship at any time and for any reason.

- The process for expressing concerns or grievances.

- The process and grounds for dismissal of a volunteer.

- The resignation procedure.

While legitimate grounds for dismissal exist, nonprofit organizations have been sued by dismissed volunteers. Therefore your organization needs clear policies and procedures in place for dismissing a volunteer.

Just as you would with a paid employee who is performing poorly, you need to document the unacceptable behaviors that lead to dismissing a volunteer. Unless the behavior is egregious, which would call for immediate dismissal, you must tell the volunteer that the behavior is unacceptable, how to correct the behavior, and the consequences for not correcting it.

Although dismissal is a perfectly legitimate step to take with a poorly performing

---

[10] Note that handling harassment allegations made by volunteers just as you would with paid staff is sound management practice, but may not always be required by law. Volunteers do not always command the same rights and protections as do paid employees.

[11] There are a number of resources for dealing with so-called difficult volunteers. See Appendix A, page 154.

volunteer, it is better both for the volunteer and the organization to negotiate a different assignment—one that more appropriately meets their needs and abilities and the needs of your organization.

I recently heard a sad story about a "fired" volunteer. He had worked in a nonprofit that delivered meals to homebound people for over twenty years and had been a gem, spreading good will and sociability to the people he visited. His driving skills weakened over time, and he had several mishaps in his car. After learning about a recent crash, the volunteer agency director told him he could no longer volunteer for the agency. He was terribly hurt and described himself as "fired from his volunteer job." The story circulated widely in the nonprofit volunteer management community and damaged the agency's reputation. Had the director considered the volunteer's needs as well as those of the agency, she might have given him a position that did not entail his driving a vehicle. But she didn't, and the agency damaged its good name and lost a valued volunteer.

External resources for use with volunteers

In many states, volunteer agencies provide information about working successfully with volunteers. These agencies can usually be found through your state's governor's office. Your local United Way may also have a volunteer center that can offer support. The Points of Light Foundation in Washington, DC is a national resource on volunteerism.

Conflict Resolution in a Unionized Workplace

If the nonprofit you lead has a union or unions, you must understand their grievance guidelines and procedures. It is also likely that the union is more accustomed to handling conflicts in a somewhat adversarial climate. This, of course, differs from the informal conflict resolution process I recommend. Recognize that introducing this means of conflict resolution is a significant change for most unions. Therefore, help union leaders understand the conflict resolution processes you plan to use in your organization. Once informed, they might be conflict managers in certain situations.

In conflicts involving union employees, follow the preliminary information-gathering steps previously discussed. After gathering information, you will need to determine if the conflict is covered by the union grievance process. If it is not, proceed with the conflict resolution process and keep the union leadership informed as a matter of courtesy.

If the conflict is covered by union grievance procedures, discuss your decision to use an informal conflict resolution process with the union steward or other appropriate leaders. Don't be surprised if union leaders resist your plan initially. Reassure them that the informal process does not eliminate the option of using the union's grievance process if necessary. (I have yet to hear of an informal conflict resolution process that closed off the option to use a union's grievance process.) Given the length of grievance processes, their formality, and their tendency to escalate relationship conflicts among parties, I hope your union leaders will be willing to try less formal conflict resolution methods first. Explain the process and show that it does not erode their authority or responsibility; it may help to make this book available to them. The more they understand about the process in advance, the more likely they are to be receptive to its use.

Having a unionized workplace affects the types of agreements parties can make. The stipulations in union contracts can limit the range of solutions in the same way that your organization's policies, procedures, and precedents can. Know the union stipulations so you can alert parties to limits the union contract imposes on their proposed solutions.

Recently, I spoke with the leaders of a large library system that was looking for help establishing an informal conflict resolution system. Five unions represented their workforce. There were so many grievances that library management and union leaders lost a great deal of time to the grievance processes. Union leaders and management alike hoped that by using an informal process they could reduce the number of time-consuming grievances and improve human relations among staff. They saw that an informal conflict resolution process might benefit union leadership, library management, and individual employees.

Conflicts Involving Harassment and Discrimination

During the information-gathering stage of a conflict, you may discover what appears to be harassment or discrimination. Because special laws and procedures apply to harassment and discrimination, you are now on a new course.

In the workplace, harassment is the inappropriate behavior of one person to another based on the person's gender, race, or disability. Discrimination involves actions or decisions that treat an individual differently from other people in the same situation, particularly if the actions or decisions stem from stereotypes or preconceptions of characteristics of the group to which that individual belongs. All acts of harassment and discrimination are inappropriate, but when made against people who are members of protected classes, such actions are illegal.

In the law, harassment is considered a type of discrimination, and both harassment and discrimination are handled by the same governmental oversight agencies.

However, the conflict management strategies for discrimination and harassment differ, so I discuss them separately. The more common of these two special cases is harassment.

Harassment

Because federal, state, and local laws govern harassment and discrimination, get the advice of someone familiar with the laws in your locality to guide you in handling a possible harassment complaint. Though there may be ordinances or regulations specific to your locale, harassment has general characteristics, and there is a general process for responding to and investigating a harassment complaint. You need to know these no matter where you work.

Harassment cannot be defined in absolute terms. However, most or all of the following elements are present in cases of harassment:

Take note!

This section is an overview of types of conflict that are governed by unique legal mechanisms—organizational personnel policies, union contracts, and state and federal laws. The information presented is meant to help you understand these situations better, but it is not meant to replace legal or other expert advice. When you embark upon handling these special conflicts, seek the counsel of experts familiar with the particular constraints, rules, and laws pertinent to your organization and the specific situation.

- The behaviors are unwanted and unwelcome. This means that the recipient does not welcome or encourage the behavior.

- The behaviors affect the workplace. Behavior can be harassing no matter where it occurs—at the work site or off-site at conferences, meetings, agency functions, parties, or other gatherings. The only criteria is that the behavior affects the workplace.

- The behaviors can be visual, verbal, or physical. Visual behaviors include posted cartoons or jokes, gestures, graffiti, or staring. Verbal behaviors include negative comments, racial, ethnic, sexual, or disability jokes, double entendres, or innuendoes. Physical behaviors include touching, rubbing, pinching, hugging, kissing, blocking someone's path, or blocking access or exit.

- The behaviors can be intentional or unintentional. The intention of the person displaying the behavior is irrelevant in determining if the behavior is harassment.

- A power differential may be present. This power differential may be between people from different hierarchical levels in the organization, or can be present when a group of employees gangs up on one person. It can also exist between people within an organization and others who have an affiliation with the organization, such as board members and staff, staff and volunteers, or staff and outside vendors or funders.

- The behaviors can be subtle or blatant. Many instances of harassment are quite subtle: comments or jokes with double meanings, or brushing or bumping against someone, which can occur accidentally. Subtle behaviors can be taken as innocent or harassing. Consequently, it can be difficult and confusing for people to assess the meaning of subtle behaviors. When behaviors are subtle, people may delay reporting harassment until a number of instances have occurred and they have determined the behavior's meaning.

- The individual who feels harassed is the person who defines whether the behavior is unwelcome or offensive. The determination of what is unwelcome or offensive lies with the person who feels harassed, without regard to the definition or intentions of the person who has offended.

    Do not use the word harassment. In its place, use the term inappropriate behavior while gathering information and discussing the issue.

There are two reasons for this. The first is that people become alarmed, afraid, and defensive when they hear the word harassment. The second is that there are many legal definitions of and rules governing harassment. It takes an expert to determine whether the particular instance you are investigating is indeed harassment. Avoid using the word at least until actual findings are made by an expert.

Following is a process to use when you suspect harassment.

1. Take action immediately

When you are alerted to a conflict that has characteristics of harassment, it is critical you take action immediately. If this
situation turns out to be a case of harassment that goes to the Department of Human Rights, the Equal Employment Opportunity Commission, or the courts, you and your organization will be judged by the following standard:

Did the management know (or should it have known) about
the harassment and, if so, did it take prompt action to stop the harassment and prevent a recurrence?

This means that even if someone tells you about possible harassment when you are in a nonwork setting or tells you in confidence, you and your organization are held responsible for taking prompt action. If, during the identification phase of a conflict, a conversation starts to sound like it might be about harassment, you must alert the person telling you that you will need to take action immediately and, while you will not needlessly identify him or her, you cannot guarantee confidentiality. You can leave it up to him or her to inform you about the situation, and as a good manager you should encourage reports of harassing behaviors. But the person reporting must understand that you, as an agent of the organization, are required to take action immediately upon learning of possible harassment.

If you discover a possible case of harassment, you must carefully document the process used to stop the harassment and prevent a recurrence. Be sure that you keep a complete and accurate written record of the investigation and actions you take. You may need this record if the complaint moves to more formal channels.

> **Steps for harassment**
>
> 1. Take action immediately
> 2. Prevent the inappropriate behavior from recurring
> 3. Prepare to collect information
> 4. Talk with the complaining party
> 5. Make a plan for further investigation
> 6. Talk with the person accused of inappropriate behavior
> 7. Work to resolve the situation

2. Prevent the inappropriate behavior from recurring

You must decide how best to stop the reported inappropriate behavior and prevent its recurrence. As an interim measure, you may need to temporarily relocate or reassign one of the people involved. If the situation involves an employee and his or her supervisor, you may need to change their reporting relationship. Depending on the situation, you may need to separate the parties. If you must, be sure the move does not negatively affect the complainant (the recipient of the offensive behavior), as this can be considered a retaliatory act by the organization. If separation needs to be made, and any sort of disruption or inconvenience results, it is best to move the person who has been accused of harassment—not the complainant.

3. Prepare to collect information

The methods for investigating possible harassment are very similar to those used during the information-gathering process in more ordinary conflicts. You want to learn the who, what, where, when, and how of the situation from all parties involved. When investigating harassment, assume the following demeanor:

- Listen carefully.
- Be friendly but businesslike.
- Withhold judgment.
- Be affirming but neutral.
- Take notes during the conversation, or write detailed notes immediately afterward. Be sure to write only information you are given and your direct observations of the person. Do not include any of your own personal infer-

ences or interpretations.

4. Talk with the complaining party

When speaking with the complainant, try to get as complete a picture of the situation as possible from his or her point of view. Questions to ask include:

- What happened (specifically)
- Who was involved
- When and where it happened
- What the alleged harasser did (exactly)
- How the complainant felt
- Whether and how the complainant responded
- If anyone witnessed the events
- If this was the first occurrence (if there were other occurrences get complete and specific details)
- Whether others have had similar experiences
- What the complainant wants to happen regarding the situation

Document all the information in careful detail. You may record your observations of the complainant's reactions to your questions—for example, if the person's face flushed or if he or she cried—but be careful to limit these notations to observable information. Do not include inferences, such as the person "seemed sad or embarrassed."

Sometimes people find it embarrassing to describe graphic details of inappropriate behavior to an interviewer face to face. Give a complainant who is having trouble describing embarrassing or upsetting behaviors the option of writing them down or describing them to someone of the same gender.

5. Make a plan for further investigation

Based upon the information you get from the complainant, develop a plan for how and from whom you will gather information. Consider how to protect the complainant's privacy with the least disruption of workplace activities. Be sure to talk with any witnesses to the behavior, others who were identified as also being recipients of the behavior, and the person or persons identified as behaving inappropriately.

When gathering information from others, you do not need to reveal identities or allegations. Be sure that people whom you interview know that though you will not identify them, you can not guarantee that others will not make their own guesses from the description of the situation.

Once again, document everything carefully. Write up each interview as completely and clearly as possible. Be sure your information is accurate and report the information you are given as well as your observations during your interview. Again, do not include your inferences or judgments.

6. Talk with the person accused of inappropriate behavior

This can be a challenging discussion. People who are accused of any inappropriate behavior usually become upset and defensive. Explain that you are gathering information, not making a judgment. Choose your language carefully. Keep your tone neutral and nonjudgmental. Avoid legal-sounding terms such as "the accused" or "harassment."

Make it clear that you are simply gathering information about an event that might be inappropriate behavior. Let the person know that you will respect his or her privacy as much as possible during the process. Gather information using the same questions suggested for interviewing the complainant. Do not provide the complainant's identity. If the person seems apt to be angry, has power over the complainant, and knows or surmises who the complainant is, warn him or her to carefully avoid any behaviors that might be viewed as retaliatory. You may need to reemphasize that you are gathering information only, not making a judgment. Use the same demeanor recommended for interviewing the complainant and others. Document the person's responses fully and accurately, without inferences or judgments.

The accusation and investigation may come as a surprise to the person accused. No matter how matter-of-fact and nonjudgmental you are, the person's first reaction is likely to be fearful and defensive. There is probably nothing you can do to eliminate this reaction completely. Surprise and concern about their employment and reputation will be uppermost in their minds.

Although it is rather limited help, be sure to give the accused person information about the process you will be following. While this does not give them any control over the events, it is somewhat reassuring for them to be informed about what to expect from the process. Keep the person up to date as the process progresses. Most importantly, remember to keep an open mind—people have been falsely accused of harassment.

7. Work to resolve the situation

Based on the information you gathered, decide whether the behavior was inappropriate for the workplace. If it was, take action to stop the behavior and prevent its future occurrence. This may involve education, a change in reporting responsibilities, or other actions appropriate to the situation. If it has not been done previously, now is the time to give your organization training about harassment. If policies exist, distribute them again. If disciplinary action is necessary, follow the guidelines in your organization's personnel code and harassment policy, if the organization has one.

If you find that a person was wrongly accused of inappropriate behavior or harassment, you still have work to do. First, the complainant may not agree and may choose to take the case outside the organization. In this case, your process and documentation will be of use and will support your organization's actions, so keep that information in a locked file until you absolutely know it is not needed.

Even if the complainant does not appeal the finding, you still have an intense conflict on your hands: Some sort of conflict likely gave rise to the initial accusation, to which a second conflict has been added. Unfortunately, the required procedure for handling harassment complaints, even when expertly managed, fuels a relationship conflict between the parties. Since the legally required process is heavily weighted toward the protection of the complainant, the accused person is often left feeling angry, alienated, embarrassed, unheard, and devalued. These feelings are often directed at both the accuser and the organization.

It takes sensitivity and delicate timing to work through this unhappy situation. I recommend that you talk in private with the wrongly accused person to discuss how to help them recover from the situation. Remember as you devise plans, they must not be strategies that could be viewed as retaliatory by the complainant.

In the ideal and in good time, helping the people with their original conflict makes sense. But in practice, I have found that people usually prefer to resolve this conflict by disengaging—having minimal contact, if any. If this is not possible, it is likely that one or both will leave your organization.

8. Steps beyond

Ideally, an organization will handle this form of conflict internally by

- Assuring that the inappropriate behavior stops and will not reoccur
- Ensuring that no reprisal or retaliation occurs
- Reasonably satisfying the complainant's fears and concerns

If this does not happen, the complainant has other more formal options to pursue. Depending on the size of the organization, the complainant may file a formal complaint with the equal opportunities officer (someone whose advice you would have sought and followed throughout the earlier part of the process). In addition, city and state agencies deal with human rights complaints. Such agencies will conduct investigations and, if warranted, mete out consequences for your organization and possible restitution for the complainant. Beyond these agencies are the courts and civil justice systems, which also hear harassment complaints.

When a complaint goes beyond the internal and informal process I have described, it is definitely time to get an expert involved (if you haven't already done so)—either an equal employment opportunity consultant or an attorney knowledgeable about nonprofit employment. This can be costly and time-consuming. But if you have carefully followed and documented the process described and demonstrated that your organization took the complaint seriously, acted promptly, and tried to protect the complainant from further harassment or reprisal, your organization should pass through the formal processes successfully.

Discrimination

As earlier described, discrimination can take the form of any action or decision that treats an individual differently from all other people in the same situation, particularly if the action or decision stems from stereotypes or preconceptions about a group to which a person may belong. There is another type of discrimination called disparate impact that needs your attention. Disparate impact occurs when an organization's decisions or policies affect people from a protected class differently than they affect other groups, for no sound business reason. For example, an organization that for no sound business reason allows some people flexible hours while holding others to strict hours might be discriminating through disparate impact. This form of discrimination is less widely known than forms that focus on race or gender, but it has important implications for how an organization develops its policies, procedures, or practices. The law's stance in regard to discrimination is the same as it is for harassment. An organization is frequently held responsible for any form of discrimination even if it was unintentional.

Protected classes of people

Because discrimination has historically been practiced against certain groups of people, various levels of government have created legislation and regulations to protect these groups. Federal laws designate the following characteristics as discriminatory if used to make decisions in the workplace: gender, race, skin color, age, religion, and national origin. Many state statutes designate additional characteristics as discriminatory: marital status, sexual orientation, creed, disability, or status with regard to public assistance. Cities may also create specific ordinances concerning discrimination. Learn the particular statutes and ordinances in effect where your organization is located. Your city and state departments of human rights can provide the information you need.

How discrimination shows up in the workplace

Discrimination in the workplace may come to light as a complaint that an individual was not promoted or given the same opportunities as a coworker. It can show up as a complaint expressed about working conditions or hiring practices. If an employee complains that they or another person are being treated differently from others in a similar situation, be alert to the possibility of discrimination.

A complaint is often the first direct sign of a conflict. In the case of a discrimination complaint, the conflict often takes the form of a process conflict; people's concerns center around the result of a decision and how the decision was made. Because the discriminatory event has usually already occurred, the resolution to this type of conflict requires determining whether the decision-making process in question was fair and based solely on factors relevant to work. The resolution of a discrimination conflict depends on the advance work an organization has done to assure that its decision-making processes are free from discriminatory practices.

Performance evaluations and hiring and promotion decisions are typical hot spots in discrimination conflicts. To protect your organization and reduce the likelihood of discrimination complaints, you need to standardize the practices, processes, and procedures used to make such decisions. The goal is to assure that all people are subject to the same criteria and treated in the same way. You need to do this preventively—after a conflict is identified, it is too late to standardize practices. The organization will be judged on the practices in place when the decision was made.

Discrimination in hiring, performance evaluation, and promotion

In hiring, protection from discriminatory practices means using a standard process for hiring employees. This means having clearly written job descriptions, selection criteria based on the requirements for successfully doing the particular job, and interview and application questions that solicit only information directly related to potential job performance. It also means not asking questions about age, marital status, religion, creed, or other personal characteristics that have no relevance to job performance. Promotion is very similar to hiring, since promotion is essentially an internal hire.

In performance evaluation, protection from discrimination means having clear performance criteria and work expectations for all employees and having similar criteria and expectations for similar jobs.

Though hiring, promotion, and performance evaluation are the most common areas in which discrimination complaints are raised, they are not the only ones. Compensation, work assignments, work conditions, training, and time off are all areas in which discrimination conflicts arise.

Disparate impact discrimination can show up in hiring, promotion, and performance evaluation when rules regarding attendance, work requirements, personnel polices, compensation, or other organizational practices are applied differently to different groups of employees in the organization. This does not mean that rules must be the same for all employees. The operative concept in the issue of disparate impact is that difference has to be based upon sound business reasons. For example, a business that is open from nine to five might require a receptionist to adhere strictly to those hours, while employees that spend after-business hours working might have more flexibility. The point is, decisions should be made with care to avoid inadvertently creating a disparate impact on workers.

Handle discrimination conflicts with care

Like harassment conflicts, discrimination conflicts are best handled internally by sensitively investigating the complaint and the processes used in making the decision in question. If discriminatory practices are found, the decision may need to be revisited and made again, and the process changed to avoid future problems.

Many of the guidelines regarding handling harassment apply to handling discrimination. Like harassment, the word discrimination elicits strong emotions. People accused of discrimination are often just as concerned, fearful, or angry as those who feel they have been its victim. Use the word cautiously. Follow the same procedures to gather information about the alleged discrimination as you would use for harassment.

External resources for handling conflicts that involve discrimination

As in cases of harassment, a dissatisfied complainant has several formal channels for his or her complaints if the organization does not respond to them. The same government agencies that handle harassment cases also handle discrimination complaints. Complainants can bring discrimination concerns to city human rights commissions and state agencies. As in the case of harassment, these agencies will investigate and determine whether discrimination occurred. They can then fine, award damages, or otherwise censure organizations found to have discriminatory practices. Although these formal processes are time-consuming and expert advice on navigating them is expensive, an organization that can demonstrate that its decision-making practices are fair and that it treats all people with the same consideration is likely to pass through the reviews successfully.

Conflicts Involving Maltreatment of Vulnerable Persons

Another situation that requires special handling is when a claim is made that a vulnerable person has been maltreated. If information about such maltreatment arises during information gathering or conflict resolution, the conflict manager must change the process.[12] If the claim is that someone connected with your organization has maltreated a vulnerable person, you will need to step in immediately to stop it. Then, handle the maltreatment claim as you would a harassment claim. (Note that conflicts not involving maltreatment can be handled using the process described in Chapter Two, often through the use of a proxy. For further information, see page 55.)

Vulnerable persons are typically defined as children or adults who by virtue of mental or physical dependency or disability are particularly vulnerable to maltreatment. All children are considered vulnerable. Often people who are elderly, physically or mentally ill, developmentally delayed, or chemically dependent are also considered vulnerable to maltreatment.

Maltreatment is typically defined as intentional or unintentional behavior that causes physical or emotional pain or injury to a vulnerable person. It can take the form of neglect, either by a caregiver or by the vulnerable person themselves. Exploitation of a vulnerable person typically occurs when they are required to render services to benefit another; it is also a form of maltreatment. So is the use of a vulnerable person's resources without proper authority, or the use of their resources to their own detriment.

Professionals who work in education, law enforcement, health care, social work, and psychology are required by law in most states to report suspected maltreatment and face legal action for not doing so. Others, while not required by law, can and should report suspected maltreatment. The laws are complex, so it is wise to contact an agency or individual with expertise if you suspect maltreatment of a vulnerable person.

In most states, you report maltreatment of a vulnerable person to the Department of Human Services or a similar department. In some states, you report to an office in county government. Check with your state government to learn where to report maltreatment of a vulnerable person.

Conflicts Involving Other Illegal Activities

Harassment, discrimination, and maltreatment are all illegal, but other crimes also crop up. The most common revolve around money—fraud, embezzlement, and the misuse of funds. Their discovery is the nightmare of every nonprofit leader.

You may discover potential illegalities in two ways: an employee may allege that another is engaged in illegal actions, or you may discover such actions yourself. In either case, your first step is to investigate, just as you would in situations like discrimination and harassment. Your investigation must be fair and impartial.

If you believe you've found illegal activity in your organization, call your attorney for advice. He or she can tell you how to proceed. Following are several questions you will want to discuss with your attorney.

---

[12] Many nonprofit organizations that regularly work with children or vulnerable adults are licensed and therefore familiar with their state laws and regulations protecting vulnerable persons. This discussion is meant for managers unfamiliar with such laws.

- Should the event be reported to the police or regulatory agencies? If so, when?

- Who should do the investigation?

- To whom will the investigator report? How should the investigator report—orally or in writing?

- What immediate actions should the organization take regarding the accused employee?

- What interim actions should the organization take regarding the accused or accuser while the investigation is proceeding?

- How can the investigation be conducted with the least disruption to the agency, the staff, and the accused person in particular?

- What steps are needed to avoid defamation and other civil claims?

Also check your organization's personnel policies, which usually have stipulations about staff involvement in illegal activities. They may state when and if you should terminate or suspend an employee involved in illegal activities. Discuss this with your attorney too. In some organizations, board policies also state how the director is to report illegal or alleged illegal actions. Your own job description may also have stipulations.

Immediately after contacting your attorney and consulting your organizational policies, confidentially alert your organization's top leaders, just as you would alert them to any other major development in the organization. Inform them about the situation, but stress that they can jeopardize the organization if they discuss it with others.

To investigate allegations of illegal activities, follow the same steps you would when investigating harassment. Remember, speak both with the persons who allege the activity and those they accuse. Keep an open mind and a nonjudgmental tone. Do not use the word illegal—simply collect information on the matter in question.

If your investigation uncovers illegal activities, you need to consider whether to report them to the police or other regulatory bodies. If the particular situation is not subject to government authority, you are not obliged to report an illegal activity; much is left to the discretion of you and your board with the advice of your attorney. Obviously, for personal and moral reasons, you must report clearly egregious crimes like murder, use of firearms, or the sale of illegal drugs—although in many cases the law does not mandate reporting.

As you and your board decide whether to report the illegal activity, consider the following:

Consider the source...

People who have been in a latent conflict (a situation in which people become increasingly distant and upset with one another before an event triggers an open conflict) often view one another as capable of immoral or illegal actions. In this frame of mind, they can easily perceive the other party's activities as illegal, regardless of the truth. You certainly want to follow up on allegations of illegal activities, but do so with an open mind. Consider whether the allegations mask some other form of conflict.

- The seriousness of the illegal activity and its effect on the organization and others
- The scope of the illegal activity—whether it is strictly internal or affects other groups or individuals
- Whether there is a pattern of recurrent illegal actions
- The victim's wishes, if there is a victim
- The relationship of the victim to the organization
- The relationship of the perpetrator to the organization
- The precedent the decision will set and its impact on the organization's future decisions
- The perception of others in and associated with the organization regarding both the illegal activity and how it is handled

In addition you will want to look at the benefits to the organization of reporting the illegality to the authorities:

- You have some control over when and how you report the situation
- Reporting is the best mechanism to avoid charges against your organization
- If the victim wants to prosecute, you may want to be the one to report the illegal activity
- Prosecution may deter others from illegal actions by demonstrating the organization will not tolerate such behavior

Not reporting an illegality also has benefits:

- Once you report, you lose control of any future investigation
- You may not want your organization's image tarnished
- The victim may not want anyone to know
- There may not be sufficient proof of criminal activity to be upheld in court
- Going to court would lead to unnecessary expenses and ill will
- There may not be sufficient interest by authorities to prosecute

Unfortunately, allegations of illegal activities are news and hard to keep quiet. (I cannot stress enough how important it is to keep information confidential. Information leaked by your organization could later become a defamation suit.) However, you need to be prepared to handle the media if the information becomes public. When you have proof of illegal activity, you many want to be the one to tell the media so that you can frame the information rather than react to the statements of less informed people.

Designate a spokesperson or spokespersons for the organization. Be sure that every person who speaks on behalf of the organization gives consistent information about the event. Make statements as simple and forthright as possible. Give information

that assures people that the situation is being handled well, but do not offer specula-
tion, unconfirmed information, or unnecessary details. Do not deny that there is
a problem or try to hide things; this piques reporters and makes your organization
look bad. Definitely consult your attorney about what information to provide. Alert
staff to channel information seekers to your designated spokesperson.

Aside from the press, other groups may be concerned with illegalities in your organization. Brief your funders, key donors, and the staff of government agencies with
whom you have major contracts. Hearing about the situation from you is infinitely
better than learning about it from the media or through the grapevine. Direct, honest, and timely communication helps retain their confidence in your organization.

Finding External Help with Conflict Resolution

Conflicts are so common that it is not feasible to get external help each time one occurs. However, you should get external help for complex conflicts or those that no
one associated with your organization can facilitate impartially.

A wide range of dispute resolution avenues are open to you. They vary significantly
in the types of issues they handle, the time and costs involved, and the amount of
control the people in conflict have over the resolution. Following is an overview
of litigation, arbitration, and meditation-arbitration (sometimes called med-arb for
short), and also an in-depth discussion of mediation, the form of external dispute
resolution I most often recommend.

Litigation

The court system is almost always available as a last
resort for settling a conflict,
but it is costly and time-consuming. Courts deal most
effectively with substantive disputes. At times they
take on process conflicts, but never relationship issues. Of the external forms of conflict resolution,
litigation gives the people in conflict the least control
over the outcome. Attorneys speak for the parties,
legal precedents and procedures shape the solutions,
and judges or juries make the ultimate decisions.
Litigation is usually adversarial, and it tends to escalate already strained relationships— often to irreconcilable levels. The system works particularly well when the
issues are substantive, stakes are high, and parties to the dispute will have no future
relationship.

Litigated disputes are heard in either criminal or civil courts. Criminal courts handle situations in which people have broken federal or state laws or city ordinances. Civil courts deal with issues of contracts and torts (personal injury claims).

Either court is accessible to nonprofits. However, court dockets are so full that judges are disinclined to deal with matters that can be handled in other venues. Frequently, the process of setting a court date drives an agreement between parties. Attorneys settle many cases through negotiations between attorneys just before the case comes before the court.

"The courts of this country should not be the place where the resolution of disputes begins. They should be the places where they end... after alternative methods of resolving disputes have been considered and tried."

Sandra Day O'Connor
Chief Justice,
U.S. Supreme Court

Arbitration

In arbitration, individuals in conflict (or their attorneys) make their best case to an arbitrator who weighs the information and determines the resolution. Arbitration can be binding, which means there is no recourse to the court system after a decision is made, or nonbinding, meaning that the parties may bring their cases to the courts if they are unhappy with the arbitrator's decision.

Arbitration is generally less expensive and time-consuming than litigation. Parties have more control, particularly if they represent themselves. The arbitration system is somewhat less formal and procedurally driven than litigation. However, many arbitrators are attorneys or retired judges, so they bring much of the litigious context and mind-set to arbitration. Information about arbitration services can be found in the telephone directory and through professional organizations of arbitrators.

Mediation-Arbitration

Mediation-arbitration, also called med-arb, is a newer avenue of dispute resolution. As its name suggests, it is a hybrid of arbitration and mediation (described in the next paragraph). It generally works like mediation, but if parties cannot come to an agreement, the mediator takes on the role of arbitrator and decides how to resolve the conflict. Many organizations that offer mediation or arbitration offer this hybrid as well, since the same professionals perform this service. The phone book and professional organizations are the best sources for this service.

Mediation

Mediation is the least formal and generally the least expensive external conflict resolution venue. In mediation, parties usually meet face-to-face to discuss and resolve their dispute with the help of a facilitator, called a mediator. (Sometimes two mediators may be called for; when mediating large groups, mediators frequently work in pairs.) On occasion, parties may bring attorneys, but usually mediation is conducted without attorneys present. Mediators facilitate the conflict resolution process, but have no decision-making authority. Mediation is effective in substantive, procedural, relationship-based, and identity-based disputes.

Because it is generally the least expensive process and one that deals with relationships in addition to substantive and procedural issues, mediation is the external system I generally advise nonprofits to start with. Mediators vary in style and quality, so it is worth doing some homework when selecting one.

Finding and hiring a mediator

Trained to facilitate conflict resolution, mediators can be found through a variety of sources. Most metropolitan phone books list community, nonprofit, and for-profit mediation organizations. Some are independent professional mediators or law firms; others are branch offices of large mediation organizations. Word-of-mouth is often a good way to find a mediator with whom you can work.

By and large, mediation services associated with law firms and large for-profit and nonprofit organizations are the most expensive. Community mediation and smaller nonprofit mediation services tend to be the least costly. Independent mediators' fees fall in between, but vary considerably. Many service providers have sliding fees, so ask if a mediator has a lower rate for nonprofit organizations.

Besides cost, consider the following questions when you look for a mediator:

Experience

- Does the mediator need special expertise or have to be familiar with certain terminology to work effectively with the parties or the type of conflict?
- Has the mediator dealt with similar situations or conflicts? Is this desirable, or would it be better if they were open-minded and had no previous involvement with the issues?

Neutrality

- Should the mediator be someone known to the parties and respected as fair and impartial or should he or she be someone neither party knows?
- Should he or she be from within or outside the community?

Role

- How does the mediator view his or her role in administering the mediation process—for example, in handling the meeting logistics, making copies of documents, or word processing?
- What does the mediator expect the parties or agency to do in the process?

Process

- What approach does the mediator recommend?

- Does this approach seem appropriate for your agency and the people involved?

Training

- How much training has the mediator had?

- Who trained the mediator?

Fees and availability

- Is the mediator available during the period needed?

- What does the mediator charge? If there is an hourly rate, what does it cover? What is the cost of time spent at mediation meetings versus preparation time or travel time?

- Can the mediator estimate the amount of time the project will require?

- Can a price ceiling be negotiated?

In some conflicts, choosing the mediator is a source of contention because each party fears that the mediator might be partial. In this case, the first step in the conflict resolution process is having the parties work together to select a mediator that all view as acceptable and neutral.

CHAPTER FIVE

Tending to the Sea
Creating an Environment for
Constructive Conflict

ONE OF THE WONDERS of the sea is its amazing diversity of life-forms. Sea worms live by undersea volcanic vents and thrive on the very elements that are toxic to us land dwellers; organisms that live without sunlight on the ocean floor create their own biochemical lanterns to light their way; huge whales survive by feeding on tiny plankton.

Among these marvels are animals that multiply by growing buds. These buds, tiny replicas of their parent, break off and become independent creatures. This is how I think constructive conflict management grows in an organization. The leaders must bring it in and nurture it, but like the sea creatures, buds of conflict management skills need to be developed and released into the cultural waters of the organization.

Previous chapters focused on how you, as a nonprofit leader, can help others resolve their conflicts. However, helping others develop their own conflict resolution skills will save you time and energy and let people use their differences in constructive ways—to gain new perspectives and understanding and to increase productivity and creativity. As conflict resolution skills flourish, divisiveness, interpersonal conflict, and hidden agendas diminish. Turf battles and daily tensions subside. Relationships with the community and service recipients deepen.

How can you go about creating this conflict-friendly environment? I recommend nine activities for creating a climate of constructive conflict in the organization:

1. Model constructive communication and conflict resolution skills.

2. Recognize the conflict resolution methods currently in place in your organization and assess their strengths and weaknesses.

3. Enrich other people's understanding of conflict, its challenges and benefits.

4. Help people in the organization gain self-knowledge as a tool for constructive conflict.

5. Encourage people in your organization to understand and appreciate differences in their histories, communication styles, decision-making methods, and cultures.

6. Offer opportunities to learn and use constructive conflict resolution skills.

7. Assess organizational systems and practices to understand their contribution to conflict.

8. Encourage and practice supportive communications methods.

9. Continually work to establish an organizational climate in which change, risk, and conflict are accepted as normal and viewed as stimulants for creativity and learning.

Tools for accomplishing these goals follow.

1. Model constructive conflict management practices.

If you have concluded that the conflict resolution methods already discussed are valuable and you are committed to "walk the talk," you have already taken the first step to integrating constructive conflict resolution into your organization. Just as your leadership underpins any cultural change in your organization, your understanding of conflict and your use of communication and conflict resolution skills are the primary factors in making these a part of your organization's culture. Seeing these methods practiced by the organization's leader is BIG. Your modeling is essential.

2. Recognize the conflict resolution methods currently in place in your organization and assess their strengths and weaknesses.

Watch carefully and think back to your experiences of conflict within your organization. What are the conflicts about? Do one or two types seem prevalent? Who are the parties in conflict? Are the conflicts within the organization or with external constituents? How are the conflicts handled or avoided? Thinking through all of these will give you a picture of the conflict resolution methods currently in use and their relative effectiveness. Note the people whose skills are strong. These are folks who can take the lead and be models for others in the organization.

3. Enrich other people's understanding of conflict and its challenges and benefits.

Early on I mentioned that conflict is commonly kept below deck. Bring the idea of creative conflict up on deck. Talk about it. Use this book and other resources to help the people in your organization understand its many shapes, the cultural messages around it, people's reactions to it, as well as the potential it holds for learning and innovation.

4. Help people in the organization gain self-knowledge as a tool for constructive conflict.

Earlier I emphasized that it is important to understand your own conflict history when you plan to help others. There are several instruments that give people insight into their own styles or preferences regarding conflict (see page 23). Each offers a somewhat different perspective, but all enhance self-knowledge. Use them as part of board orientation and staff development activities; they contribute to people's understanding of themselves and each other.

5. Encourage people in your organization to understand and appreciate differences in their histories, communication styles, decision-making methods, and culture.

Because we are each familiar with only our own way of processing information and coming to decisions, it is easy to forget that other people perform these activities differently. It is common for people to view others who have different styles as incompetent, weird, or worse. This misperception is often at the core of workplace conflict. When people with significantly different styles are interdependent, as in the workplace, they can get frustrated or angry that things are not being done in ways that make sense to them. They often begin to psychologically distance themselves from their "different" coworkers.

This is how latent conflict starts. People accentuate their differences, withdraw, and become more and more judgmental about one another—until some straw or other breaks the camel's back. I have come to greatly value the Myers-Briggs Type Inventory (MBTI) as an important and credible tool for understanding my own perceptions and those of others—and as a result, for preventing the development of these sorts of conflicts.[13]

The MBTI, first and foremost, helps people understand their own unique way of processing information and making decisions. It also helps them recognize the

---

[13] Some people are wary of the MBTI because it has been misused to pigeonhole people or make excuses for inappropriate or incompetent behavior. However, it is an excellent tool when administered and analyzed by appropriately trained people. The MBTI has a long history of research and has high credibility as a reliable assessment. In addition, in the past few years the inventory has been further refined, so that its new version, the MBTI Expanded Analysis Report (EAR) gives a deeper look at people's perceiving and decision-making preferences.

different ways in which others do these things. When colleagues understand their own ways of thinking and value other people's ways, some conflicts are eliminated altogether and people are better prepared to use their differences constructively.

The MBTI must be administered by a certified trainer. After the inventory is explained and administered, it is sent to a national center for analysis and then returned to the trainer. He or she will meet once with your organization to administer the inventory and a second time to return the results to participants and explain the results. All individual inventories are confidential and private, so individuals can choose whether to share results. Regardless of whether inventories are shared, participants learn a lot about different ways of thinking.

Besides using the MBTI and related instruments, you can help change the culture of your workplace by helping people recognize the role of family history, ethnic background, and religious heritage in shaping perception. The exercises in Chapter One, "How did you learn about conflict?" (page 21), "Understanding cultural contexts," (page 29) and "Mixed messages" (page 33) can be used with groups to help them understand the role of family, culture, and communication styles in shaping personal perceptions of conflict.

6. Offer opportunities to learn and use constructive conflict resolution skills.

As you become comfortable and confident as a conflict manager, consider moving your organization to the next stage by empowering others to do the same. Information about conflict and conflict resolution skills can become part of your staff and board development activities. When the people working in your nonprofit have these skills, you will find everyone's time better used. You can actively turn potentially destructive conflict into creative and constructive problem solving. Less time is lost through positioning, scheming, and rumormongering.

The skills presented in Chapter Four of this book should ideally be in every person's communication tool bag. The information and exercises that accompany the sections on affirming and restating, mirroring, asking neutral questions, assisting upset people, identifying interests, reframing issues, limiting blaming and belittling by using structured statements, and breaking stalemates are helpful to staff at all levels of the organization. Having people practice makes them more likely to use the skills when conflicts arise. These skills can be taught in various ways ranging from formal training sessions to informal discussions at staff or board meetings.

7. Assess organizational systems and practices to understand their contribution to conflict.

Organizational systems can create both intentional and inadvertent conflict. Systems of checks and balances that distribute authority and assure quality control can become arcane and destructive over time. Review systems as your organization grows to see that the checks and balances do not create conflicts beyond those needed to assure quality.

Areas to review include budgeting and other resource distribution systems (like space and personnel allocations), performance appraisal systems, and program evaluation systems. Personnel policies—especially those regarding hours of arrival and departure, notice of intended absence, and general office decorum—should also be examined. Such rules often remain after the original conditions that triggered their creation have changed.

Most policies and procedures relating to these systems are established to reduce the level of risk to the organization. Therefore, you will need to assess the risk aversion built into these systems and determine how much risk your organization can afford to take. Many conflicts occur when people in gatekeeping roles such as legal, personnel, and finance staff, who frequently need to say "no," become enamored of rules and forget to assess the risk of following old rules in a changed environment. Rethinking old policies and procedures needs to be done with these staff, but this is no easy task. Gatekeeping is often a form of power, so you need to prepare for potential resistance and power struggles.

8. Encourage and practice supportive communications methods.

The organization's communications style is a key clue to how safe conflict is. This cultural characteristic can range on a continuum from defensive to supportive.

When an organization's chief style of communication is defensive, people anticipate critical responses. In office meetings and conversations, defensive communicators make evaluative and judgmental statements much more often than descriptive statements. They are likely to attribute problems to individuals rather than situations, and to describe problems in terms of the person or group "at fault." In organizations with defensive communication, statements are either ambiguous, leaving loopholes for the intimidated speaker, or else certain and dogmatic, leaving no room for disagreement. Lastly, defensive communication is at work when individuals in groups allude to their status or formal position as justification for a point they are making.

All of these practices make people feel wary as they communicate. The defensive style gives people the clear message that it is unacceptable and unsafe to address conflict directly. As a result conflicts go underground, becoming personal vendettas, hidden agendas, and increasingly fierce turf wars.

In contrast, supportive communication styles tend to be more descriptive than evaluative. Problems are attributed to situations and not to people, statements are clear and leave room for alternatives, and people de-emphasize formal power relationships and communicate with mutual respect and empathy.

Take a fresh look at the types of communication occurring in your organization. You will quickly get a sense of whether your organization's climate is one in which people feel safe to address conflict directly and constructively. While you alone can't change your organization's culture, you can model supportive communications and work to make the organization a safe place for constructive resolution of conflict.

9. Continually work to establish an organizational climate in which change, risk, and conflict are accepted as normal and viewed as stimulants for creativity and learning.

"One does not discover new lands without consenting to lose sight of the shore for a very long time."

Anonymous

Management gurus preach the benefits of every organization becoming a learning organization, thriving on chaos, managing in white water, and making everyone in the organization entrepreneurs. Of course, these conditions make conflict more likely! Creating an organizational climate in which change, reasonable risk, and conflict are embraced is a wonderful ideal. But doing it takes time, patience, and the willingness to reconsider many traditions. Change is unsettling, and, especially in larger organizations, staff are used to these so-called paradigm shifts blowing in like a nor'wester and blowing out in short order. Don't be in a hurry. Slowly and steadily steer your organization toward this ideal culture by making small and easy changes first.

Look long and hard at your organization's real incentives and disincentives for bringing conflicts above deck. What incentives or disincentives are built into your reward and recognition systems, your human resources systems, your performance appraisal systems? Who gets promoted, rewarded, and challenged? How well are your "different" people accepted? Are their ideas really considered? Are people rewarded for taking the risk of addressing conflict, or does the risk simply mean more work for them with no rewards? What happens to risk-takers when they "fail?" What messages do other members of the organization get about people who are willing to call a conflict a conflict? What messages do people get when they are in conflict? What attitude does the organization have toward outsiders—those people who are either genuinely outside the organization, or who are pariahs within the organization? (More often than one would hope, nonprofits assume a fortress mentality, guarding against outsiders, whether they are squeaky wheels from inside the organization or outspoken members of the external community.)

In addition to considering the formal systems that tell people if conflict, change, and innovation are acceptable, you will want to assess less formal systems. These include how authority is used and the role of friendship and interdependence in your organization.

When people in an organization decide how to address conflict, they combine their understanding of the conflict, their personal ways of dealing with conflict, and the unspoken organizational norms and rules about conflict.

Organizations that emphasize formal authority tend to be less hospitable to constructive conflict resolution. When people assess the risk of addressing a conflict, they consider the organization's messages about authority. If these include "don't bother the boss," "make the boss look good at all costs," "do what you're told; don't ask why," or "don't bring bad news—messengers get killed," people will be afraid to point out a conflict, let alone address it. Changing the way authority is viewed and used in an organization is a huge challenge. It often takes a change of leadership to make this happen.

The level of interpersonal friendship and support among people also affects how conflict is handled. In a friendly and psychologically safe environment, people are much more confident that a conflict can be raised and resolved in constructive ways. Though you certainly can't create friendships in the workplace, you can set a tone that supports their development by encouraging informal gatherings and letting employees know that a certain amount of workplace chat is fine. Similarly, you can support interdependence—a sense of group identity in the organization that encourages constructive conflict resolution. When friendship and interdependence thrive, people feel safer about airing conflicts.

Playing in the Waves

Surfers are gleeful when they learn that a storm at sea is creating high surf. They grab their boards and race to the shore to play in the waves. Those crashing walls of water look truly formidable to a landlubber, but for folks who understand and know how to use their power, the waves are nature's playground—an exhilarating amusement ride that tests their skills and grants a great sense of mastery.

Conflict, too, appears as a storm at sea—generating waves of emotion and ideas that threaten to throw us painfully against the rocks of blocked desires or wash us away from what is near and dear. My hope in writing this book has been to offer both knowledge and skills that will enable you to ride—and help others ride—conflict's waves to constructive ends. I hope that this information allows you to respect and harness the storms of conflict, but not fear its waves.

"Anything worth doing is worth doing wrong for a while."

Anonymous

Just as the most skilled surfers expect to tumble, you can expect that everything will go not perfectly. This means climbing aboard again when you have lost the momentum of the wave, or were toppled into its curl. You will need agility, patience, stamina, and a genuine sense of optimism. Each ride has its lessons and each builds understanding, skill, and mastery for the next set of waves.

This book has focused largely on conflict within nonprofits. But there is another and wider arena in which this information and set of skills are useful. As nonprofits increasingly work with organizations from other sectors to solve community problems, differences in values, procedures, and styles will invariably arise. These differences hold great potential for creating conflict. Making that conflict constructive will not only enable different organizations and sectors to work together, but will stimulate innovative ways to address our communities' problems. Those of you who have been involved in collaborations and partnerships among nonprofits already know how challenging they can be. As these collaborations cross business and government sectors, conflict management skills will be even more essential.

Conflict is as inevitable as the pounding surf and as broad as the sea. Like the sea, it can be either destructive or life-giving. I hope this book will help you bring new life and creativity to your organization and its mission. Like the great sailors who marry wind and water into speed, I hope you experience a sense of challenge, mastery, and exhilaration as you navigate the seas of conflict.

APPENDICES

Appendix A: Recommended Reading and Bibliography

Appendix B: Worksheets and Conflict Resolution Forms

Appendix A: Recommended Reading and Bibliography

Recommended Reading

The publications described below have been especially important in the development of my work on conflict management. I have categorized them as works on conflict, creative thinking, cultural differences, and miscellany. These works are also listed in the bibliography.

Conflict

Constantino, Cathy A. and Christina Sickles Merchant. *Designing Conflict Management Systems.* Explains how to set up conflict resolution systems within organizations. This practical book marries organization development theory with conflict management theory. I recommend it for those leaders who want to foster a conflict-friendly organization.

Crum, Thomas. *The Magic of Conflict.* Focuses on the constructive outcomes of conflict.

Folger, Joseph, et. al. *Working through Conflict.* Explains the many aspects of conflict and offers a means to analyze it. The book has a strong communications emphasis.

Moore, Christopher W. *The Mediation Process.* Offers in-depth analysis of negotiation processes and explanations of conflict resolution techniques used by professional mediators. Many of these techniques are transferable to conflict resolution by organizational leaders.

Stulberg, J. B. *Taking Charge: Managing Conflict.* Delineates the different roles a manager can assume when confronted with conflict.

Creative Thinking

Coleman, Daniel, Paul Kaufman, and Michael Ray. *The Creative Spirit.* Gives numerous ideas for creativity in many settings.

DeBono, Edward. *Serious Creativity.* Explains the author's theory of creative thinking and provides many tips and exercises to stimulate creativity.

Ford, C. and D. Gioia (eds.). *Creative Action in Organizations.* Offers a series of essays by academicians and organizational leaders about creativity in the workplace. Their introduction and synthesis of the ideas within the varied essays is very informative.

Cultural Differences

Axtell, Roger E. *Gestures*. Offers information about the meaning of nonverbal communication around the world.

The David M. Kennedy Center for International Studies. *Culturagrams*. Short monograph series gives specific cultural information about 143 different cultures. They are published by Brigham Young University, PO Box 24538, Provo, UT 84602

Gudykunst, William B. and Young Yun Kim. *Communicating with Strangers*. Sets a basic framework for effective cross-cultural communication.

Hall, Edward and Mildred Hall. *Understanding Cultural Differences*. Noted anthropologist couple explains how culture is transmitted and how it impacts human behavior.

Tannen, Deborah. *You Just Don't Understand: Women and Men in Conversation*. Covers communication styles across gender.

Miscellany

Mackenzie, Marilyn. *Dealing with Difficult Volunteers*. Covers many different types of challenges one faces when working with volunteers, including conflicts and "firing" volunteers.

Myers, Isabel Briggs. *Gifts Differing*. Explains the Myers-Briggs Inventory and value of each psychological type profiled by the inventory.

Bibliography

Adams, J. *Conceptual Blockbusting: A Guide to Better Ideas*. San Francisco: W.H. Freemen and Company, 1974.

Angelica, Emil and Vincent Hyman. *Coping with Cutbacks: The Nonprofit Guide to Success When Times Are Tight*. St. Paul, MN: Amherst Wilder Foundation Publishing Center, 1997.

Axtell, Roger E. *Gestures: Do's and Taboos of Body Language Around the World*. New York: John Wiley & Sons, 1991.

Barret, Susan L. *It's All in Your Head: A Guide to Understanding Your Brain and Boosting Your Brain Power*. Minneapolis: Free Spirit Publishing, 1992.

Barron, Frank. *Creative Person and Creative Process*. New York: Holt, Rinehart & Winston, 1969.

Broom, M. and D. Klein. *Power: The Infinite Game*. Amherst, MA: HRD Press, 1995.

Bush, Robert and Joseph Folger. *The Promise of Mediation: Responding to Conflict Through Empowerment and Recognition*. San Francisco: Jossey-Bass, 1994.

Carse, James. *Finite and Infinite Games*. New York: The Free Press, 1986.

Coates, J. *Men, Women and Language*. London: Longman, 1996.

Coleman, Daniel, Paul Kaufman, and Michael Ray. *The Creative Spirit*. New York: Dutton, 1992.

Constantino, Cathy A. and Christina Sickles Merchant. *Designing Conflict Management Systems*. San Francisco: Jossey-Bass Inc. Publishers, 1996.

Crawford, M. *Talking Difference: On Gender and Language*. Thousand Oaks, CA: Sage Publications, 1995.

Crum, Thomas. *The Magic of Conflict*. New York: Simon & Schuster, 1987.

Dacey, J. *Fundamentals of Creative Thinking*. Lexington, MA: Lexington Books, 1989.

The David M. Kennedy Center for International Studies. *Culturagrams*. Provo, UT: Brigham Young University, 1999 (annual series).

De Bono, Edward. *Lateral Thinking: Creativity Step by Step*. New York: Harper and Row, 1970.

De Bono, Edward. *Serious Creativity*. New York: HarperBusiness, 1992.

Delpit, L. *Other People's Children: Cultural Conflict in the Classroom*. New York: The New Press, 1995.

Devine, E. and N. Braganti. *The Traveler's Guide to Latin American Customs and Manners*. New York: St. Martin's Press, 1988.

DeWine, S and R. G. Ross. *Communication messages in conflict*. Management Communications Quarterly, 1: 389-413, 1988.

Eisner, R. *The Chalice and the Blade: Our History, Our Future*. Cambridge, MA: Harper & Row, 1987.

Evarts, W., J. Greenstone, G. Kirkpatrick, and S. Leviton. *Winning through Accommodations: The Mediator's Handbook*. Dubuque, IA: Kendall/Hunt, 1992.

Fisher, James C. and Kathleen M Cole. *Leadership and Management of Volunteer Programs: A Guide for Volunteer Administrators*. San Francisco: Jossey Bass, 1993.

Fisher, Roger and S. Brown. *Getting Together: Building a Relationship That Gets to Yes*. Boston: Houghton Mifflon Company, 1988.

Folger, Joseph, M. Poole, and R. Stutman. *Working through Conflict: Strategies for Relationships, Groups, and Organizations*. 3rd. ed. New York: Longman, 1997.

Ford, C. and D. Gioia. *Creative Action in Organizations: Ivory Tower Visions & Real World Voices*. Thousand Oaks, CA: Sage Publications, 1995.

Forrester, M. *Psychology of Language*. Thousand Oaks, CA: Sage, 1996.

Gadlin, Howard. *Conflict resolution, cultural differences and the culture of racism*. Negotiation Journal, Jan. 1994, p. 33.

Gardner, Howard. *Creating Minds: An Anatomy of Creativity Seen Through the Lives of Freud, Einstein, Picasso, Stravinsky, Eliot, Graham, and Gandhi.* New York: Basic Books, 1993.

Gorden, William. *Synectics: The Development of Creative Capacity.* New York: Harper, 1961.

Gudykunst, William B. and Young Yun Kim. *Communicating with Strangers: An Approach to Intercultural Communication.* Reading, MA: Addison-Wesley, 1984.

Hagberg, Janet. *Real Power: Stages of Personal Power in Organizations.* Salem, WI: Sheffield Publishing Company, 1994.

Hall, Edward and Mildred Hall. *Understanding Cultural Differences.* Yarmouth, ME: Intercultural Press, 1990.

Hall, Edward. *Beyond Culture.* Garden City, NY: Anchor Press, 1976.

Hall, Jay. *Conflict Management Survey.* Monroe, TX: Teleometrics International, 1969.

Hall, Peter D. *Inventing the Nonprofit Sector and Other Essays: On Philanthropy, Voluntarism, and Nonprofit Organizations.* Baltimore: Johns Hopkins University Press, 1994.

Harman, Willis. *Global Mind Change: The Power of the Last Years of the Twentieth Century.* Indianapolis: Knowledge Systems Inc., 1988.

Harman, Willis and H. Rheingold. *Higher Creativity: Liberating the Unconscious for Breakthrough Insights.* New York: St. Martin's Press, 1984.

Hawley, J. *Reawakening the Spirit of Work.* New York: Simon & Schuster, 1995.

Heider, John. *The Tao of Leadership: Lao Tzu's Tao Te Ching Adapted for a New Age.* Atlanta: Humanics Ltd., 1985.

Henderson, G. *Cultural Diversity in the Workplace: Issues and Strategies.* Westport, CT: Quorum Books, 1994.

Herrman, M. (ed.). *Resolving Conflict: Strategies for Local Government.* Washington, DC: ICMA, 1994.

Hirsh, Sandra K. and Jean M. Kummerow. *Introduction to Type in Organizations.* Palo Alto, CA: Consulting Psychologists Press, 1989.

Hocker, Joyce and William Wilmot. *Interpersonal Conflict.* Dubuque, IA: Wm. C. Brown Publishers, 1991.

Hofstede, Geert. *Cultures and Organizations: Software of the Mind.* New York: McGraw-Hill International, 1991.

Howard, P. *The Death of Common Sense: How Law Is Suffocating America.* Thorndike, ME: G.K. Hall, 1995.

Kilmann, Ralph and Kenneth Thomas. *Thomas-Kilmann Conflict Mode Instrument.* Sterling Forest, NY: Xicom, 1974.

Koberg, D. and J. Bagnall. *Universal Traveler: A Soft-System Guide to Creativity, Problem-Solving, and the Process of Reaching Goals*. Los Altos, CA: William Kaufman Inc., 1974.

Kochman, Thomas. *Black and White Styles in Conflict*. Chicago: University of Chicago Press, 1981.

Kreidler, W. *Creative Conflict Resolution: More Than 200 Activities for Keeping Peace in the Classroom*. Glenview, IL: Good Year Books, 1984.

Kritek, Phyllis B. *Negotiating at an Uneven Table: Developing Moral Courage in Resolving Our Conflicts*. San Francisco: Jossey-Bass, 1994.

Land, George and B. Jarman. *Breakpoint and Beyond: Mastering the Future Today*. Champaign, IL: HarperBusiness, 1992.

Lewis, Flora. *Europe: A Tapestry of Nations*. New York: Simon & Schuster, 1987.

Lohmann, Roger. *The Commons: A New Perspective on Nonprofit Organizations and Voluntary Action*. San Francisco: Jossey Bass, 1992.

MacKenzie, Marilyn. *Dealing with Difficult Volunteers*. Downers Grove, IL: VM Systems-Heritage Arts Publishing, 1988.

MacKinnon, D. *The Creative Person*. Berkeley: Institute of Personality Assessment, 1961.

Mayer, Bernard. *The dynamics of power in mediation and negotiation*. Boulder, Au:

Moore, Christopher W. *The Mediation Process: Practical Strategies for Resolving Conflict*. San Francisco: Jossey-Bass, 1986.

Morgan, Garret. *Images of Organization*. Beverly Hills, CA: Sage Publications, 1986.

Mortensen, David. *Miscommunication*. Thousand Oaks, CA: Sage, 1997.

Myers, Isabel B. *Gifts Differing*. Palo Alto, CA: Consulting Psychologists Press, 1980.

Nachmanovitch, Stephan. *Freeplay: The Power of Improvisation in Life and the Arts*. Los Angeles: Tarcher, 1990.

Parnes, Sidney. *Source Book for Creative Problem Solving: A Fifty Year Digest of Proven Innovation Processes*. Buffalo, New York: Creative Education Foundation Press, 1992.

Prince, George. *The Practice of Creativity: A Manual for Dynamic Group Problem Solving*. New York: Harper & Row, 1970.

Putnam, L. and C. E. Wilson. *Organizations communication conflict instrument*. In M. Buroon (ed.). Communication Yearbook 6:629-652. Beverly Hills, CA: Sage, 1986.

Osborn, Alex. *Applied Imagination: Principles and Procedures of Creative Problem Solving*. New York: Scribners, 1963.

Rahim, M. S. *A measure of styles of handling interpersonal conflict*. Academy of Management Journal, 26: 368-376, 1983.

Russel, Peter. *The White Hole in Time: Our Future Evolution and the Meaning of Now.* San Francisco: HarperCollins Publisher, 1992.

Schellenburg, J. *The Science of Conflict.* New York: Oxford University Press, 1982.

Sternberg, Robert. *The Nature of Creativity: Contemporary Psychological Perspectives.* New York: Cambridge University Press, 1988.

Stewart, E. and M. Bennett. *American Cultural Patterns: A Cross-Cultural Perspective.* Yarmouth, ME: Intercultural Press, Inc., 1991

Stulberg, J.B. *Taking Charge: Managing Conflict.* New York: Free Press, 1987.

Tannen, Deborah. *Gender and Discourse.* New York: Oxford University Press, 1994.

Tannen, Deborah. *You Just Don't Understand: Women and Men in Conversation.* New York: Morrow, 1990.

Ury, William, J. Brett, and S. Goldberg. *Getting Disputes Resolved: Designing Systems to Cut the Costs of Conflict.* San Francisco: Jossey-Bass, 1988.

Vaill, Peter. *Managing as a Performing Art: New Ideas for a World of Chaotic Change.* San Francisco: Jossey-Bass, 1989.

Van Gundy, A. *Techniques of Structured Problem-Solving.* New York: Van Nostrand Reinhold, 1988.

Von Oech, Roger. *A Kick in the Seat of the Pants: Using Your Explorer, Artist, Judge, & Warrior to Be More Creative.* New York: HarperCollins Press, 1986.

Von Oech, Roger. *A Whack on the Side of the Head: How to Unlock Your Mind for Innovation.* 2nd ed. New York: Warner Books Inc., 1983.

Walker, D. *The Effective Administrator.* San Francisco: Jossey-Bass, 1979.

Weaver, Gary (ed.). *Culture, Communication and Conflict: Readings in Intercultural Relations.* Needham Heights, MA: Gim Press, 1994.

Wheatley, Margaret. *Leadership and the New Science: Learning about Organization from an Orderly Universe.* New York: Berrett-Koehler, 1992.

Wolfgang, Aaron. *Everybody's Guide to People Watching.* Yarmouth, ME: Intercultural Press Inc., 1995.

Appendix B: Worksheets and Conflict Resolution Forms

Electonric versions of these worksheets may be downloaded from the publisher's web site. Use the following URL.

http://www.wilder.org/pubs/workshts/pubs_worksheets1.html?069164

These worksheets are intended for use in the same way as photocopies, but they are in a form that allows you to type in your responses and reformat the worksheets. Please do not download the worksheets unless you or your organization has purchased this book.

Fill out this worksheet for each person involved in the conflict.

Name:

Expressed Positions

Expressed Interests (mark key interests)

Interests you inferred (mark key interests)

(continued)

Gender, cultural, and racial differences to consider

Emotional state

Power

    a) **Types of power available**

    b) **How has this person used power in the conflict**

How does this person describe the conflict?

What assumptions is this person making about others in the conflict?

Group the individuals you listed in Worksheet 1 into parties with similar positions and interests. Note their positions, interests, power relationships, and emotional states.

Party 1:

Position	Interest	Power	Emotional State

Party 2:

Position	Interest	Power	Emotional State

(continued)

Now list those people indirectly concerned with the conflict.

Concerned Person:

Position	Interest	Power	Emotional State

Concerned Person:

Position	Interest	Power	Emotional State

Concerned Person:

Position	Interest	Power	Emotional State

Finally, list all the interests identified by all people grouped by parties (if possible). Note if these interests are substantive, procedural, relationship-based, or identity-based. Mark their key interests.

Interests–Party 1:	substantive	procedural	relationship-based	identity-based
Interests–Party 2:				
Interests–Party 3:				

First, review the checklist for screening whether a conflict is appropriate for informal conflict resolution processes.

1. **Are there allegations of harassment or abuse? (If answer is yes—use other established processes.)**

2. **Is there evidence of criminal activity? (If answer is yes, consult attorney to determine action to take—in some cases, conflict resolution processes are still appropriate.)**

3. **Are vulnerable persons involved (children, elderly, mentally retarded, mentally ill, etc.)? (If so, consider whether appropriate support and process design will facilitate an informal conflict resolution process.)**

Second, review the characteristics of the conflict.

4. **Is there a union contract that has bearing on this conflict?**

5. **Does the conflict seem to be interpersonal or is it induced by the system—or is it both? (Describe)**

(continued)

6. Does the conflict seem to take any of the classic shapes as discussed in Chapter One on pages 18-20? These shapes—direct conflict, spiral conflict, subtle conflict, and violent conflict—may give you clues to yet unidentified issues.

7. Are there currently known limitations to potential resolutions that you must impose on behalf of the organization?

8. Who is the most appropriate person to facilitate the conflict resolution process?

Agreement to Participate in a Conflict Resolution Process

The parties below acknowledge and agree that they are willing to participate in a conflict resolution process in order to attempt to resolve the issues raised in a dispute about

_____ .

(a one-sentence, very general description of the conflict)

The parties also acknowledge and agree to the following ground rules:

1. Attendance at Meetings: The parties will attend scheduled conflict resolution meetings.

2. Good Faith: The parties agree to negotiate in good faith. They may refuse to divulge information, but will not give false information and will tell the truth as best they know it. They will agree only to resolutions with which they genuinely believe they will comply.

3. Conflict Manager: The conflict manager does not represent any of the parties. The role of the conflict manager is to promote and facilitate voluntary resolution of the above-referenced issue. He or she has no duty to provide advice or information to a party or to assure that a party has an understanding of the problem and the consequences of his or her actions. The conflict manager will remain impartial and neutral toward the parties. The conflict manager will not discuss the process or disclose any communication made during it to any persons, with the exception of reporting abuse of a vulnerable person or threats of bodily harm.

4. Confidentiality: All discussions and observations made during conflict resolution meetings will be privileged and confidential. No document produced or verbal disclosure made in the conflict resolution process that is not available through another readily available source will be discussed with others outside of the conflict resolution meetings nor will such documents or disclosures be admissible as evidence at any subsequent legal actions. Such documents may be made public only through signed agreement of all parties. Exceptions to this include maltreatment of vulnerable persons, harassment, discrimination, and illegalities. Such situations may require processes different from this informal one.

5. Respectful Behavior: The parties agree to discuss their issues using respectful language and behaviors.

The parties and others participating in the conflict resolution process hereby voluntarily sign agreement and affirm that they have read it.

Conflict manager/s

_____   _____

Parties

_____   _____

_____   _____

Dated: _____

Note: Any agreement entered into by a person with authority to act on behalf of the nonprofit may create a binding contract.

Letter of Understanding

The undersigned parties, after participating in a conflict resolution process about the issue(s) of

_____.

(a one sentence, very general description of the conflict)

have mutually developed and agreed upon the following means to resolve their conflict:

_____

_____

_____

_____

_____

_____

_____

_____

_____

_____

_____

_____

Conflict manager/s

_____   _____

Parties

_____   _____

_____   _____

Dated: _____

Note: Any agreement entered into by a person with authority to act on behalf
of the nonprofit may create a binding contract.

Process Steps Checklist

When you meet with each person in the conflict, you will need to describe how the conflict resolution process works. Also repeat this explanation at the beginning of the conflict resolution meeting between the two parties. People need to hear the rules twice, once in private, so they can express all their doubts, concerns, and questions, and once at the beginning of the meeting. The repetition reminds the participants of the steps they will follow and assures each person that the others have been advised of the same steps and ground rules.

---

1. The conflict resolution meeting will open with the conflict manager welcoming people and introducing them, if necessary.

2. The group will discuss comfort issues and logistics, including location of bathrooms, refreshments, seating, time limitations, and dates for future meetings.

3. The conflict managers will discuss the process and ground rules:

   - The goal and benefits of the conflict resolution process

   - The conflict manager role as impartial facilitator and as the organization's steward

   - Expected decorum

   - Confidentiality and concept of good faith

   - Alternatives to this process

   - Use of caucus

   - How the meeting will proceed

   - The role of outsiders (trusted friends and advisers) in the resolution meeting (if any are used)

   - Questions about ground rules

   - Any additions to ground rules as discussed and agreed to by all parties

4. The parties will make an oral or written agreement to participate and follow ground rules.

5. The conflict manager will briefly and generally describe the conflict as he or she understands it.

6. Each party will tell their understanding of the conflict.

7. The parties and conflict manager will discuss and clarify their understandings of each others' perspectives on the conflict.

8. The parties and conflict manager will identify the key interests and establish an order in which to discuss them.

9. The parties will generate ideas for solutions to key concerns.

10. The parties will evaluate solutions in the light of the interests they've identified.

11. The parties will select mutually agreeable solutions.

12. The parties will discuss implementation, monitoring, and follow-up to the solutions.

13. The parties and conflict manager will fine-tune and write up the agreed upon resolution.

14. The conflict manager will initiate a way to celebrate the resolution.

15. The conflict manager will assure follow-up.

Index